Gesture of Balance

A Guide to
Awareness, Self-healing, and Meditation

Tarthang Tulku

DHARMA PUBLISHING

Nyingma Psychology Series

Illustrations:
Page 171: Dorje Legpa, a protector of the Buddhadharma
Page 173: Stupa, a symbol of pure awareness

ISBN: 0–913546–17–8; 0–913546–16–x (pbk)
Library of Congress Number: 75–5255

Typeset in Fototronic Elegante
Printed in the United States of America
by Dharma Press

Eighth Printing, 1988

Contents

Foreword

The essays in this book are unusual in the sense that they present Buddhist ideas and perspectives without indulging in theories about Buddhism. The very fact that we in the Western world speak about Buddhism as if it were a rigid system, that can (and maybe should) be dealt with in abstract terms, shows how little real understanding of a different set of values exists even at the present time. These values are inherent in a person's life and are not merely arbitrarily assigned to it.

The following essays address themselves to the living person, not to an abstraction or a shadowy image; and they do so in terms which a living person can understand intellectually as well as feel deep within his heart. That is why these essays are unusual—they are not simply props or pegs on which to hang one's preconceptions, but stimulants to reconsider and to reassess the situation in which we find ourselves; and through this re-awakening to what is at hand, we are stimulated to set out on the path toward growth and maturation.

Although each essay is self-contained, in their totality they reveal a steady progression. The starting-point is honesty—honesty toward ourselves as being part of a wider life-stream and as sharing in its vicissitudes, not as being detached onlookers. As participants of an ever-widening life-stream we will not be able to grow when we struggle against it, when we build up tensions and blockages, but only when we learn to relax so that the stream can flow calmly in us. Relaxation thus becomes the indispensable prerequisite for meditation which is a 'tuning-in' to the life-stream and not the build-up of new fixations, even if they are advertised as a cure-all. Meditation in this sense of 'tuning-in' leads to a heightened awareness in which the artificial boundaries of a subject and an object are transcended in a unitary awareness that heals the festering wounds of our dividedness against ourselves. Lastly, as participants we are linked to those who went before us and to those who will come after us. We have received meanings and values from our fore-bears and we work over and re-interpret this heritage and hand over the emergent patterns to our descendants. Whether or not what we transmit will live on depends upon our honesty, the point from which we set out.

If these essays are unusual because of their direct-ness, so also their author is revealed in a fresh light. In the same way as we tend to create an abstraction of what actually is a concrete message and a practical application, so we also tend to create an image of a man and, in believing in the validity of the image, to forget the real person. Man can never be defined in rigid terms. He is more like a crystal shining in many colors. The title *rin-po-che* means 'preciousness', and the preciousness of a crystal lies in its many facets. In these essays we discover a very important facet of Tarthang Tulku Rinpoche—his warm-hearted humanness. Maybe it is this facet or aspect of his that has to be emphasized over and again because only too often we forget our and others' humanness and lose ourselves in mere abstractions and fanciful images. It is this humanness that makes the essays all the more significant and places their author firmly in the on-going ever-fresh tradition and transmission of Nyingma teachers and thought.

HERBERT V. GUENTHER

Head of Department
of Far Eastern Studies
University of Saskatchewan

Preface

This volume offers some introductory discussions of basic practices in meditation and awareness as they relate to present-day life in America. I have given many such talks to my students over the past seven years, and it was recently suggested that I share these ideas with a wider audience. Certain themes in these chapters overlap to some extent, but this repetition is intended to provide a foundation for developing an increasingly deep understanding.

Although the ideas and practices which are presented here are specifically oriented to the experience of Western people, they are founded on and reflect the many different stages and paths of the Buddhist tradition as preserved by the Nyingma lineage.

The first and most basic theme emphasized by Buddhism concerns confronting life directly—taking stock of our experience honestly, without being limited by small-minded or sentimental fantasies. Each person must recognize the essential problems and values of human life, so that the proper direction can be taken. A person at the Hinayana stage recognizes that impermanence and frustration are central features of life which must be honestly faced and dealt with. It is understood that each person must take responsibility for overcoming the frustrations of life and for cultivating those qualities which are most central to fulfillment as a human being. Individual effort is called for, rather than a passive appeal for salvation at the hands of another.

Such a mature and realistic attitude is complemented by the Mahayana focus on compassion for others and on a profound understanding of the nature of phenomena. The Mahayana insight reveals that all experience, however constricting or frustrating, is still open in an essential way, and therefore we do not need to seek our individual escape from it. Compassion for others springs naturally from this insight, since our own position is no longer seen as so limited, insecure, or frustrating. We become more concerned with the difficulties of others, and can afford to try to help them. Since this type of compassion is based on understanding rather than on sentimental projections, it is generally appropriate and helpful.

Historically, Buddhism has developed various schools and teachings in order to meet the needs and abilities of different types of people. These schools have perfected many meditative techniques to help clarify and cope with the problems of life, and to help us get in touch with profound and valuable aspects of our bodies and minds. Buddhist meditation practices are always related to practical assessments and to the essential energies and qualities of human experience. And a strong foundation and balanced orientation is needed in order to progress from basic, preliminary practices to deeper meditative experiences.

For those who have thoroughly implemented the orientation of the Hinayana and Mahayana teachings, Buddhism traditionally offers the Vajrayana as the continuation and final 'path'. The Vajrayana is not a limited doctrine or approach, but rather a path of infinite growth. It completely transcends all dualistic meditations and all conceptualizations. In the Vajrayana, life is seen not as a problem to be resolved, but as an experience that bears infinite richness and creative energy. Nothing is rejected or repressed, since the practitioner of the Vajrayana develops sufficient skill and sensitivity to relate to the beneficial aspect of all existence.

The profound and sensitive nature of the Buddhist teachings was carried to Tibet from India in the eighth century by Shantirakshita and by Padmasambhava, the greatest Vajrayana master of the period. Both teachers are closely associated with the Nyingma or 'Ancient Ones', the first of the four major lineages of Tibetan Buddhism.

The Hinayana, Mahayana, and Vajrayana teachings are all contained within Nyingma and are presented in forms that are both flexible and true to the deepest intentions and experiences of each path. Nyingma translations and commentaries based on the Indian texts were made with great attention to the lived significance of each term and idea, so that in carrying these teachings into a new language, such as English, they readily relate to modern life and concepts.

In Tibet, the Nyingma followers interacted with many different types of people—not concentrating on an ex-

clusively monastic orientation—and Nyingma masters
have always included people of different attainments and
life-styles. When presenting these ideas in America, I
have tried to retain this adaptable and open-minded
character, and therefore hope that the present volume
can offer something of value to people of different positions and interests. My main concern is that the discussions help people to establish a path of growth that is
right for them, so that they may take care of themselves
in the midst of a troubled world. My lectures do not have
a very intellectual or elegant style, but as one of my
teachers once said, "Of what importance is lofty speech,
if simple speech can get the ideas across?"

I am extremely grateful to all my friends in America
who have aided me in my work, and especially to my
students, for their many efforts on my behalf. In particular, I would like to thank Judy Robertson and Debby
Black for their help in editing these talks, Rosalyn White
for illustrating them, and all the staff of Dharma Press for
producing them.

I dedicate any benefit deriving from this work to the
people of America, and am deeply thankful for having
the opportunity to preserve and share with them the
Nyingma tradition.

TARTHANG TULKU

Head Lama of the Tibetan
Nyingma Meditation Center
and the Nyingma Institute

Part One

OPENING

Impermanence and Frustration

*People are willing to go to war
and even give up their lives for a cause,
but they cannot give up
the causes of their suffering.*

I mpermanence is the essence of our human condition. It controls much more than just our lives; it holds sway over the entire cosmos—all the stars and planets, as well as our earthly environment. We can see the effects of impermanence by watching the rise and fall of nations, of our society, and even of the stock market. Impermanence permeates all existence. We can see the changes in our lives and the lives of our friends and families, but the most devastating change in human life—death—is always catching us by surprise.

In this society almost everyone is afraid of death—but to appreciate life fully, we have to face reality. Impermanence and death are integral parts of being alive; this realization can vibrate within us and wake us up . . . we see that although our lives are very dear to us, they do not last forever. To be born a human being is a very rare privilege, and it is important that we appreciate our lives and take advantage of this opportunity.

With an understanding of impermanence, many aspects of life that one ordinarily finds fascinating no longer seem so appealing. We become able to see *through* them and find that they are not actually that satisfying. We can then more easily let go of our attachments and fears, as well as our own little shell of protection. Thinking about the impermanence of life wakes us up; we realize that at this very moment we are actually alive!

Still there is struggle, for we find ourselves wanting things that we know will cause us pain or frustration. Our habit patterns are very hard to break, and even when we try, obstacles always seem to appear—our desires and attachments push us to repeat the same destructive patterns. Our emotional needs habituate us not only to material things, but very subtly to our self-identity. We do not want to lose our sense of control over ourselves, our environment, or even over other people. But until we let go of our attachments to personality and self-image, it is difficult even to see these life patterns, let alone to change them.

Because there are certain attitudes and preferences that we do not like to let go of, we continually get involved in difficult situations and experience inner conflicts. Sometimes we can give up important things —our money, our homes, or property—without much difficulty. But emotional attachments—such as to praise and blame, gain and loss, pleasure and pain, or kind and harsh words—are very subtle. They are beyond the physical level; they exist in the personality or self-image, and we are not willing to let them go. We also have certain attitudes and prejudices, usually hidden, that we do not even like to acknowledge. Our attachments have a magnetic pull which holds us in one place as if we were in prison. It is hard to tell whether this controlling force comes from our past actions or from our fear of death or from some unknown source; yet we cannot move—so all kinds of frustrations and conflicts attack us, creating more frustration and pain.

People are willing to go to war and even to give up their lives for a cause, but they cannot give up the causes of their suffering. It is mysterious how certain psychological fixations dominate us so strongly that we cannot give them up—even when we understand intellectually the pain they carry with them. We ask ourselves, why is this? Why do I need to hold so tightly to these patterns and habits . . . these attitudes . . . this particular self-image?

We can observe our life-patterns carefully, and come to accept how even the most subtle graspings and negativities cause us to suffer. As our understanding and awareness grow, we see the importance of working through our emotions, attachments, and negativities, and we also see that the ultimate solution comes from within. Then when we truly wake up to our painful condition, we can begin to change our innermost attitudes, and some real progress can be made. Although often it is difficult even to recognize what is healthy or wholesome because our environment and daily experience are so artificial, when we finally decide to act in a healthy and balanced manner, our lives naturally fall into this new pattern. We do not even need to leave our homes and families to effect these changes—for the changes are within us.

We are usually taught that to be 'spiritual' means to reject the world. But even a spiritual person can live comfortably, enjoy his work, take care of a family, and be successful in society and in the world. We are also taught that we should not be selfish. But we actually can be 'selfish' in taking care of ourselves—not in an egotistical, grasping, or melancholy way, but in a deeply caring way—by making our bodies and minds as harmonized as possible. When we carefully observe our senses and feelings, we learn to accept and appreciate ourselves, and to be open to others. Through the integration and balancing of our minds and bodies, it is possible to attain the inner peace and joy which itself is love.

But usually we just continue to follow the same negative patterns, seldom finding satisfaction, because we do not truly enjoy any given moment. We are often uncomfortable in the present and feel distressed because whatever is happening is a little unexpected. We find it difficult to relate to situations openly or directly. The problem is that by focusing on the past or future, we never fully deal with the present, and thus it can never truly give us satisfaction. We are always expecting that in the future there will be something greater, higher, deeper, or more fulfilling. So we may never be particularly happy or satisfied, because our whole lives consist of endless preparations: for family life or love affairs or various entertainments.

Our time is usually divided between work and pleasure. In fact we work, in part, to prepare for pleasure —we are always looking forward to entertainments, to weekends, or to vacations. But do we find real pleasure in these pastimes? Are they really worthwhile? Is it not possible for us to learn to look within and appreciate ourselves, rather than continuing to look outside ourselves for fulfillment? When we find inspiration, openness, and balance within, then our lives become genuinely happy and worthwhile—we can then find happiness even in our work. Instead of wasting our energy and human potential in useless thoughts and actions, we begin to act constructively, for the basis of the spiritual path is the development in ourselves of what is truly balanced, natural, and meaningful.

We can begin by accepting each moment and enjoying it, but most of us do not know how. Enjoying life may be extremely important to us, yet too often when we experience pleasure, our minds project the satisfaction into the future, so our lives become filled with empty dreams that never materialize. It is difficult to truly accomplish anything in the present when our minds are always oriented toward some future goal.

This does not mean that we should avoid making intelligent plans for the future; it only means that we must live more fully in the present. When we endeavor to develop ourselves in the present, we will grow toward our future goals until they are accomplished. The present naturally leads us to the future, and the future changes according to how we live in the present. When we are confident in whatever we do, and all our actions are meaningful, then not only our daily lives, but our future lives as well, will be balanced and harmonious.

When we open ourselves to our present experience, we can realize that *right now* we can enjoy our lives . . . right now we have the opportunity! We do not need to be too concerned with the future—the present will lead us there no matter what we do. But much of the time, because our awareness of the present moment is dull or unclear, it seems that something is going on in the shadows, behind our consciousness, and we just drift and follow it. Meanwhile, time and energy are lost and we may be unaware of what happened yesterday, this morning, or even this afternoon; we are unaware of much of what is happening in our lives. And when we think about it, we may find that we are basically unaware of how we became who we are today. When we were children we looked and talked in certain ways; how did we change? It is difficult to trace the transition. We can follow some of the experiences we have been through, but it is surprising how many things we do not remember—or remember inaccurately—for it is like trying to recall last night's dream. And that is how we live our lives!

I n certain areas of our lives, where selfishness motivates us, such as perhaps in our business or profession, we can be very sharp, clever, and clear-minded. But in other areas of our lives, we have no goals, no purpose, no aim, and our awareness seems very fuzzy or vague. When we look back on the child that we were, is this what we would have wished for him? We are hardly aware of what is happening around us or within us, and at times we are little more self-sufficient than a two-year old. Often we work and act in certain ways only because that is what is expected of us . . . we imitate others in our jobs and our relationships; for it is very difficult to make our own decisions, particularly when we have no overall perspective on our lives. Unconvinced that *this* is reality, we have not yet awakened to the present, and thus are not able to determine what is important, or *why* it is important. After a while we may even stop caring and just let go of everything . . . but we are not really 'letting go'; we are just giving up in despair.

There are two kinds of 'giving up' or 'letting go'. There is giving up attachments, and there is giving up because of difficulties and disappointments. The person who has inner strength and openness does not 'give up'—but gives up grasping and attachment, and consequently gains freedom and confidence. Because he has no attachment to being a certain way, but simply follows the truth within his heart, no obstacle or disappointment can overcome him. The person who gives up because he cannot control his life or manage for himself does not *fully* give up; he maintains a certain determination to continue on, but does not have the strength or courage to follow his inclinations—he just gives in to whatever is happening. As he is not able to give up his grasping and negative emotions, it is not clear to him which way is right and which way is wrong—so he suffers in indecision. Although he does not necessarily undergo physical pain, he undergoes psychological suffering—the pain of not being able to grasp what he desires. The craving for sensation dominates him, and he is divided within himself.

Suffering does not come only from physical pain—it can occur when certain inner attitudes are imbalanced or out of harmony. When we undergo great conflict or pressure, making even a simple decision can be very difficult. Our awareness can become so limited that we even experience 'gaps' in our memory. Even when we manage to make a decision, we may suffer if we do not achieve all we hoped to accomplish. And when we succeed at something, we may become proud and attached to it, then suffer through our fear of losing it. Or perhaps we become very tense in attempting to reach some goal or in trying to materialize some hope or expectation. We feel frustrated because we never get enough of what we want, whether it be approval or love, attainment or success. No matter which way we turn, there is conflict and indecision; we are caught in between and do not know which way to go.

These uncertainties create continual disturbances within us, and our minds become like internal clocks on which the hands continually move around in circles without ever halting to point the time. Finally, we become incapable of making any decisions, going completely blank and having no specific thoughts or direction; we just become passive and uncaring, in a cycle of despair. And we can continue on and on in this way indefinitely.

Because our powers of self-observation are usually not well developed, we are often blind to our suffering. We have to be able to look inwardly to discover the subtleties of our present experience, and this we find difficult to do. Therefore, it is perhaps easier to learn from past experience, for although it is often difficult to learn from suffering at the time it occurs, when we re-enter our feelings of the past, we can sometimes see them with more clarity and detachment.

Most of us experience a great deal of suffering in our lives as we go through cycles of stress, dullness, and restlessness. We try to escape this suffering, but it always returns. Yet when we have the strength and courage to look deeply into ourselves, into our pain, we see a strange paradox. Even when we want to give up suffering, it seems that we are not ready—we hold tightly to it.

But eventually, as we become more familiar with our pain, we may firmly decide that we do not want to suffer any more. At that point we let go of our suffering and wake up—there is an inward change, and we clearly see

the foolishness of the countless self-tortures we have created for ourselves. This inner change is the real learning process.

Most of the time, we have trouble accepting what seems like interminable suffering in the world, yet in a sense, suffering is one of the best teachers. Through sensitively observing the patterns of our pain and suffering, we can learn to understand ourselves physically, emotionally, and mentally. Ideas often have little connection with our lives, but to have pain and to feel it—that is the source of genuine learning.

Frustration and suffering lead to a deep understanding of ourselves and to the realization that there is no way to escape pain except by going through it and beyond it. When we are comfortable, often we are not even interested in looking any further—but the more frustration, pain, and confusion we feel, the more urgently we seek a way out of it. Suffering itself does not ultimately give us any answers, but it may inwardly push us to wake up—to begin meditation, to develop our awareness.

Suffering, then, can be seen as a positive experience, because it gives us the opportunity to transform our emotions and bring ourselves closer to liberation. When we realize this we can wake up and find inner strength and energy which will sustain us each day throughout the rest of our lives.

There is a Tibetan saying that a person who does not remember impermanence or the inevitability of his death is like a queen. In ancient times, within the royal courts, a queen had to maintain an image of poise and self-confidence, and she had to be very concerned about protecting her reputation and self-image. But in her heart, she had all kinds of desires and fears—of the king's pleasure or displeasure, of power, or the loss of her position. So her poise was essentially a pretense in order to protect herself.

Similarly, we may dedicate our lives to a spiritual path in an external sense, yet underneath, we may still have many desires—for power, or position, or praise. We do not remember impermanence or the certainty of death, and so we cannot protect ourselves from our desires. But when we realize the impermanence of our lives, we can adapt ourselves more readily to all situations and not become attached to or dragged down by them.

When we contemplate death, we can see death itself as a natural transition—not necessarily an ending—but a continuation. In terms of time, the moment of death is the present and our experience of this life is the past. Death, or present experience, is an invitation to the future, not an ending in any sense. For those who are accomplished in meditation, death is seen as an opportunity to achieve a very beautiful experience—or even liberation from all suffering.

But most of us look upon death as a loss rather than an opportunity—we are afraid of the loss of our egos. We feel the same sort of fear when we give up our attachments and habit patterns; we may be frightened or confused because we are not certain 'who we are' without them. At this time each experience may be actually fresh and new, but we may not be prepared to live without our habitual ego-protections.

When we keep the fact of our death in mind, it can give us a kind of 'charge'—something inside of us clicks, inspiring us to do something constructive with our lives. Each moment becomes very important. We realize that however long we have left to live, we will spend a third of that time sleeping—and then we have to eat three meals a day, spend time talking, working, dealing with emotional problems—and fit in all the other activities that make up our lives.

In carefully charting how we spend our time, we can see that we have little time left for utilizing positive energy to help either ourselves or others. Therefore, it is important to set up a structure or a life pattern for ourselves. Self-discipline is essential if we are going to learn to lead constructive lives, free from the turbulence of our emotions, negativities, and pain.

It is also helpful to periodically test our concentration and awareness. Whenever we are caught in a physical or mental conflict, we can focus on it, heat it up, go into the center of it. The way we react in such situations is a good indication of the strength of our awareness. We may be able to retain our tranquility in most circumstances, but experiencing and transcending upsetting situations can be very difficult. Yet without this ability, we will continue to experience much pain and frustration, not only in this life but in the period after death. For although this life can give us situations that are difficult to deal with, the state after death is a far greater test of our strength and awareness.

Even if we observe ourselves carefully, we can never be sure when we will die. When we go to sleep at night we cannot be certain that we will wake up; when exhaling a breath, it may sometimes happen that our breath will not return. Even our attempts at pleasure—drinking, smoking, taking drugs, or going for a drive—could be the cause of our death. And, even health food will not keep us alive forever. So it is very hard to predict how much longer we have to live.

Therefore, it is important to begin now to balance and motivate our lives, for when we grow old, our senses fade . . . our eyes cannot focus well and our taste is not so keen. Friends often no longer respond and, because of our age, society may not pay much attention to us. Thus, we may no longer feel part of the community. It is very rare to see a young man and an old man together for long—they usually have very different interests and energies; and since there is so little communication, the old ones among us often become very isolated and alone. But each of us will become old . . . we cannot escape it. Time passes quickly and we may deeply regret it if we miss the opportunities we now have to make our lives meaningful. So often we hear older people say, "I wish I had heard this twenty years ago," or "I have wasted all these years and now it is too late." Of course, it is never too late—but we do not know how much time we have left. So why do we not begin now?

These ideas may seem very simple, but they are part of a long, historical tradition that has made life meaningful to people for many generations. From time to time, we can remember to be grateful that we are alive and have the opportunity for inner growth. As for frustration and impermanence—we can be grateful that they are there to wake us up. There are difficulties to face in our lives, but when we are strong and confident, we will realize our own potential. Little by little, we can contact our own inner awareness, and take courage and confidence in our realizations.

The more we think about the pervasiveness of impermanence and of the insubstantiality of whatever we wish to hold onto, the better understanding we have of our tendencies toward fascination and grasping. Consequently, we find that we are not so easily distracted and do not become so quickly caught up in just whatever happens next. We may even experience a whole re-ordering of the priorities in our lives. As we begin to gain greater understanding and compassion, our lives become more cheerful and filled with positive energy, which can be of help and inspiration to others.

Frustrations are life's gestures
Through which we grow in knowledge,
And impermanence is the circular turning of our lives,
Experienced as a play in which meaning is unfolded as balance.

Beginning with Honesty

*We are afraid to learn
because we are afraid to grow and
to assume the greater responsibility
that goes with growth.*

One thing we can be sure of: We do not know everything. We have no certain knowledge of the past from which we came or the future to which we are proceeding. We may not even know the present condition of our bodies, minds, and feelings. Because our understanding is so limited, we have to deal with an underlying anxiety—a suspicion that we are caught in our own ignorance. There may be a sense of a reality beyond the screen of our daily lives, but this truth is somehow hidden from us.

Our experience has given us *some* knowledge, yet, at the same time, we seldom honestly look at what we know. A particular action might be clearly advantageous, but often we choose to do the opposite, if it is easier or less demanding. And then we make excuses for our choice. Objections, opinions, and judgments occur in our minds to prevent us from positive action. Often when we attempt to do what is beneficial, we strengthen our insecurities by suggesting to ourselves that what we are doing is not right; we may criticize ourselves so continuously that eventually we retreat in the opposite direction, refusing to face ourselves.

So two factors are present: one, that we do not know certain things, and the other, that we do know some things, but we do not want to admit to ourselves that we know them. Even when we actually see a situation clearly, we often try to interpret it to our advantage, and consequently we cheat ourselves. Our spiritual strength may not be powerful enough for us to actually face reality, so we forget what we know or refuse to look; we become lazy or turn our minds to other matters. We do this knowingly. So we find ourselves caught in these two destructive patterns: ignorance and avoidance.

The underlying cause of these patterns is fear, incessant fear caused by lack of inner strength. This fear divides our attention and motivation and thus interferes with our ability to see ourselves clearly. Fear is one of the ego's mightiest weapons for self-preservation, because once feelings of fear, inadequacy, and weakness occur, we do not want to face the reality of ourselves or our own lives.

We thus learn to hide our true thoughts and feelings so that the way we talk, look, think, feel, and act are not genuine. We cover up our feelings about ourselves and others, not wanting to realize that we are so far from genuine understanding. If anyone dared to suggest that our egos were playing games and that we were wasting our lives, we would find countless excuses to defend ourselves. But when we observe carefully, we have to admit that often we hide from ourselves. We may feel so threatened that we find it easier to constantly deny the need for change than to actually change—even though underneath we realize what we need to do to make our lives meaningful and worthwhile, and how to go about it. Basically, we are just too weak to begin.

Since childhood, we have learned from friends and family how to play 'games'. We play games for two reasons: the first is our need to survive socially and economically, and the second is our ego involvement —we want to be accepted. When we are skillful in following the social rules, we play well and have successful lives, but we may never touch the deeper levels of our hearts. Often we get so involved in our games that we can no longer distinguish ourselves from them, and in this way we lose contact with our inner natures. We may even become physically or mentally sick from always grasping and struggling. But although we become extremely tired of playing games, still we play them— with friends, with family, with society. We may even *know* we are playing games, but our circumstances create tense or pressured situations which seem to prevent us from acting in accordance with our inner guidance.

So it is helpful to observe our egos and watch how cleverly we play games—and whether we play successfully or not. In professional circles, where everyone understands the rules—playing games is acceptable, even respectable . . . admirable when done cleverly. Everyone knows how to manipulate others, how to be shrewd and slippery, how to make things smooth on the surface while hiding things underneath. There are all kinds of games, and almost everything is somehow involved in one type of game or another. The attitude is, "How do I win, no matter what!" No one seems to care if someone or something is damaged or destroyed in the process. All that matters is winning.

Yet even when we are successful, the pressures from our obligations can cause our physical and mental energies to tighten so much that they seem to hold us in bondage; we may even feel that our personal relationships are constricting. The pressures, disappointments, and fears begin to limit our ability to work creatively and effectively; yet we do not know how to break free. In every direction we see pain, loneliness, and confusion— until we long to escape. Trying to avoid the situation, we go on trips on the weekends and in the evenings we plan entertainments. Still our mental pain and inner restlessness continue. Although we are reluctant to believe that our own actions and attitudes have been the cause of our pain, eventually we cannot ignore this conflict. Finally in desperation we realize that we must change.

Perhaps we decide to follow a path of inner development, but we waver, feeling that we must first finish our work—*then* we will give up our job or position, *then* we will practice. And in the end, we simply never get around to it. We may have many beautiful dreams, yet we accomplish very little in our entire lifetime, either spiritually or materially. People everywhere in the world spend their lives dreaming of developing spiritually without ever doing much about it. But particularly in this country, very strong will power is needed in order to develop internally. We get caught in competition for the vast stores of untapped power which modern technology has made available to us. We live under intense pressure to conform to the rules and restrictions of our 'civilized' urban society. The structure is organized in such a way that, if we do not conform, it is difficult to survive. Thus, many of us are uncomfortable, yet only a few of us are able to make the decision to change our lives, and fewer still have the will power to do it.

Therefore, even if we start on a spiritual path, it does

not mean we will continue. This is not because an impossible discipline is required, but because we lack courage and confidence. We ignore our abilities and potential for developing the personal power that we need for going through ego-breaking experiences. Consequently, although many of us try to discover truth, very few succeed.

This does not imply that spirituality has no power to help us, or that there is something wrong with the teachings or our ability to understand them. The problem is that maintaining a spiritual attitude is very different from our habitual way of thinking—and we find ourselves caught in conflict between the two. Our senses attract us to the worldly way, but our intellect and intuition urge us to follow a spiritual path, because it is ultimately more satisfying and meaningful. So we try to walk two paths that are in conflict with each other. Or we may proceed along a spiritual path for awhile, but then run into difficulties. Our fantasies and expectations are not fulfilled, or we think we have learned enough and so we revert to our old way of life. There we may still find many of the problems and habits we thought were left behind. The difference between our expectations and experience can cause us to feel that the time we spent on a spiritual pursuit was wasted. Yet when we follow only a material path, we eventually experience a sort of spiritual hollowness which we cannot ignore forever.

Once we begin to change, it is difficult to return to our former way of life, even if we want to. Something is awakened inside of us, and the positive force of change creates a momentum which impels us to continue. Then we discover that the spiritual path is *right here,* whatever we are doing; we may not have been able to walk the path deliberately, so the path came to us.

Even if we try not to believe that the continual round of desiring and grasping is destructive, our disappointments and frustrations will eventually sober us and help us face the realities of our lives. So no matter what hardships or obstacles we have to face on the spiritual path, we should not give up—for if we do, we will just have to face the obstacles again later. Everything, ultimately, is our own decision; but if we vacillate back and forth, undecided, we are just wasting valuable time. We need to decide now to face our lives honestly.

We are constantly trying, either directly or indirectly, to protect our egos and self-images; this habit is one of the hardest to give up. We may wish there were a way to develop inwardly without hurting the ego, without analyzing, meditating, and persevering. We would all really love it if we did not have to work on ourselves. But unfortunately, without removing our obscurations and becoming clear-sighted, it is not easy to progress. Even when we think our minds are clear, they may actually be frantic, cloudy, or filled with feelings of 'lostness'. Sometimes it seems that we just do not want to see. And if this is the way we are, how can we wake up from this dream?

Very accomplished teachers look upon all living beings with great compassion, because they see how exhausted beings are by constant grasping. Most of us have little meaning or direction in our lives; all we want is to satisfy our desires, be comfortable, feel happy and relaxed, or be very excited and sensual. We may have many such wishes, but these pleasures consume our energies like a flame attracts and consumes a moth. Unaware that craving and attachment give no lasting

satisfaction, we create even more pain for ourselves
—and then we fight to hold on to the cause of our own
suffering. We become like an old toothless dog in a
Tibetan village that gets hold of a bone and chews on it
until his gums bleed. Tasting blood he thinks, "Ah, how
juicy and tasty this bone is!" Even when we know that
there are actions more worthwhile than our attachments,
we continue to play games with ourselves and let our
egos dominate us. Now that we have the opportunity to
break our habit patterns, why do we not care enough
about ourselves to admit our games and change? Why do
we continually try to fool ourselves?

We are afraid to learn because we are afraid to
grow and to assume the greater responsibility that
goes with growth. On the surface we may think we want
to learn, but on deeper, more subtle levels, growth and
change threaten us. So, although we constantly try to
improve ourselves and our relationships—to feel more
joy and to be more positive—our actions are scattered,
and we attain few results. For example, we decide we are
going to meditate: we make all sorts of preparations
—arranging the room, lighting incense—then we sit
down and give ourselves directions: "I will be silent,
perfectly relaxed and aware . . . without grasping or
holding thoughts." But throughout the time of meditation, we play an elaborate game. We seldom keep our
minds on the present moment, but busy ourselves with
past memories or future plans—or we may simply fall
asleep. Even after years of study and discipline, we do
little but continually prepare and instruct ourselves—
trying so hard that we never truly begin.

Nevertheless, experience is an excellent teacher; we
can learn a great deal from all the suffering, frustration,

and confusion we go through. Finally, we will become so exhausted by our self-deceptions, graspings, and negative emotions that we will change automatically. But first we need to recognize and understand the results of our actions. Even after our lives are over, these results continue; so if we do not remove the poisons now, there is no way to avoid more suffering in the future. We will continue to be caught between the two extremes of grasping and suffering, in the multi-level cycle of past regrets, future hopes, and present confusions. We need tremendous courage to accept our pain and confusion, for all this time we have created and encouraged our suffering and at times we even like it! It seems we are not *ready* to walk away from suffering. We continue to make mistakes, create confusion, and accumulate frustration. The ego plays many games with us and permeates all our feelings, sensations, and ideas; yet we are not even truly aware of how the ego creates these patterns in our lives or how our various negative attitudes and motivations develop. All we know is that we will continue to suffer from our pain and problems until we are exhausted.

We need to honestly observe our daily lives and directly confront our weaknesses and problems. Whether we call this a spiritual path or religion is not important; what matters is that our actions are straightforward and our minds are free from playing games. If we are honest and sincerely love the truth, we can revolutionize our lives. We do not need to blindly follow a particular system, but can develop in our own way by listening to our hearts and following the truths we discover in our own experiences. Totally committing ourselves to finding truth can be a positive, powerful step.

Regardless of our past, we can now make a choice for our future. If we are determined to work on ourselves honestly and intelligently, much worthwhile growth can take place. Honesty is required because we have to learn to take care of ourselves in the best possible way; intelligence is required because there are many obstacles to overcome. Unless we are relentlessly honest, ultimately we will cheat ourselves by trying to cover up our mistakes or trying to escape our difficulties, rather than confronting ourselves and bringing about meaningful change. If we want to attain inner peace and balance, we must begin with honesty.

Taking Responsibility

*Ultimately there is no way to escape
taking responsibility for ourselves.*

We all wish to be happy, to live full and worth-while lives—yet life does not have much meaning if we wake up most mornings worried and anxious, and spend our days feeling frustrated or useless. We can perhaps find temporary relief in various forms of ego gratification, but eventually we realize that such pleasures are fleeting. If instead, we learn to take responsibility for ourselves, and to live in balance and harmony, we will experience a deep sense of inner freedom which will give purpose to our lives, and sustain us through even the most difficult of situations.

When we carefully observe every aspect of our bodies, minds, and feelings, and everything that happens to us for just one day, we will be able to see and even to predict the patterns, attitudes, and qualities that will continue for the rest of our lives. In looking at the way our time is spent, we often find that because we do not schedule the things we want to accomplish, though the day seems busy, much of it is spent in confusion and daydreaming. We may even wander about, with nothing specific to do—no purpose and no plans.

Each day is a link in the chain that makes up our lives. So, on a practical level, we should always be aware of what we are doing, not in order to become rich and powerful, but to live in the most balanced way possible and to enjoy being alive.

We have a rare opportunity in this golden land to be self-sufficient, to be generous, and to burden no one. Taking care of ourselves is not so difficult when we have an open and willing attitude. If we were responsible for 200 or 300 people's needs, we might have problems; but it is not that difficult to take care of only one person. We weigh just 100 or 200 pounds and stand only five or six feet high, yet most of our problems are in our heads, which are only eight inches wide—and this we find hard to take care of!

Many of us did not learn how to be responsible when we were growing up, and the knowledge gained in ten or fifteen years of schooling often does not have much value on a practical level. So we find that as adults, we do not know how to lead balanced and meaningful lives. Even though we consider ourselves self-sufficient and responsible, unless we understand the hold the emotions and the ego have on us, we may only be deceiving ourselves. The moment we face a crisis, we learn whether or not our inner strength is sufficiently developed to carry us through our difficulties.

Sometimes we try to fight our problems indirectly, blaming others for our troubles. This leads to confusion and creates a thick, negative atmosphere within and around us. Although it is easy to criticize others, facing and overcoming our own weaknesses and mistakes is much more difficult. So, we tell ourselves that our problems will solve themselves if we can 'just get away' for awhile; or perhaps we think we can escape from our problems and the problems of others by following a spiritual path. But ultimately there is no way to escape taking responsibility for ourselves.

When we learn to deal directly with our complaints and difficulties, romanticized ideas about the spiritual path are no longer meaningful. We see that what is important is to take responsibility for ourselves, and to always be aware of our thoughts, feelings, and actions. We *can* deal effectively with our problems, develop our potential, and discover meaning and value in our lives. This may sound simplistic, but it sometimes is helpful to just forget our problems for a short time. In the process we see that much of what we have been so caught up in has narrowed our perspective. Our worry, anxiety, and unhappiness have themselves become an obstacle to our inner balance and development and have prevented us from dealing constructively with our difficulties.

Emotional cycles and habit patterns are difficult to break, for our mental confusion often makes it hard to distinguish what is healthy from what is harmful. This is particularly evident where people live in crowded conditions and are exposed to diverse and conflicting influences; the confusion and negativity can be overwhelming. People develop a sense of hopelessness—a feeling that there is no alternative, no way out. Eventually, such an attitude causes loss of vitality and total indifference.

Therefore, it is important to recognize the power of our emotions—and to take responsibility for them by creating a light and positive atmosphere around ourselves. This attitude of joy which we create helps to alleviate states of hopelessness, loneliness, and despair. Our relationships with others thus naturally improve, and little by little the whole of society becomes more positive and balanced.

In watching our emotions, we see how they are contagious. When someone is laughing, we feel like laughing; when someone is crying, we too feel sad. The same is true when someone is depressed. Negativity is like an infectious disease—when one person is negative, then others also become agitated and negative.

So let us take the time to develop awareness, to freshen our minds and our senses . . . for we cannot afford to waste time being sad, emotional, or confused. At this very moment, we can begin to take responsibility for ourselves. These are not ideals or goals for some future time. We can start right now.

Life is constantly moving, continually changing— one moment passes, leaving another, which is never the same as the last. Every moment our bodies go through physiological and psychological changes of which we are unaware. When we are conscious of these changes, we can more easily appreciate life and communicate with others. However, when we are unaware of what is happening in our lives, we may suddenly realize that our lives are half over—and we have made little progress in freeing ourselves from our obstacles or in developing our positive qualities. Because life is constantly moving—much faster than a river—we need to use each moment well.

It is important, then, to be aware every moment—to first look and think about what we are doing—and not to act heedlessly. The spontaneity that comes from certainty and self-confidence is a very positive quality; but so often when we respond without thinking, we are like a piece of cotton that flies wherever the wind takes it. Spontaneous action is often unpredictable, and thus can result in confusion or bewilderment; we can be carried to extremes by our cloudy minds. So we need to control our impulsiveness and depend instead on inner strength and conviction. Still, most of us prefer to follow whatever fascinates us at the moment, without considering the consequences.

Once there was a monkey king who looked down the walls of a canyon and saw the bright moon reflected in the water. "Oh, what a beautiful jewel—I must have it!" he thought. When he told this to the other monkeys, they all said that it would be very hard to obtain; but the monkey king said, "I have an idea: one monkey will hold onto a tree and everyone else will form a line, each one holding tightly to the tail of the monkey in front. Then we can lower our monkey chain down to the water and the last one will be able to reach the jewel. So five hundred monkeys dangled one by one down to the water, but the weight of all the monkeys was too much for the one holding onto the tree, and all five hundred monkeys fell into the water and drowned.

Our minds are often like the monkey—when we do not carefully consider our actions beforehand, we will be unable to clearly see the consequences, and our jewel-like fantasies, dreams, and selfish graspings will cause us trouble. When our actions are done blindly, with no practical or logical direction, we may get trapped in situations which are even more enmeshing than our present circumstances.

So be aware of your body and senses. Come out of the fog of dreaming of the future or reliving past memories. Give up emotional romanticism and just be conscious of what is happening in your mind and in your feelings. Once you find your balance, you can maintain it, no matter what happens in your life.

The patterns of your daily life can be your education. From time to time analyze your thoughts and examine the events of your life; and practice being aware every moment. When you do this steadily each day, you will develop a healthy quality of genuineness; your life will become less chaotic and confused, and you will not be so interested in looking for satisfaction outside yourself. Facing each situation with awareness—is one of the best ways to take responsibility.

Opening the Heart

*Once our hearts are open, all existence
appears naturally beautiful and harmonious.*

The basic teachings of the spiritual path arise from within our hearts. When our hearts become our teachers and give us confidence, spiritual nourishment flows through the heart center and releases healing energies. At that time other enjoyments and sensations seem, by comparison, like momentary flashes. So it is important to contact our hearts and listen to our inner silence.

Often, however, our study or meditation contacts our thoughts and feelings only superficially. We do not accept ourselves for what we are, but spend our lives dreaming and grasping for pleasures outside ourselves. These fantasies hypnotize us and prevent us from touching our innermost feelings—feelings which then become covered with layers of disappointment created by our unfulfilled expectations. Fantasizing thus creates a rift between our minds and bodies.

Life seems rather empty when our hearts are closed.

We may read books, ask advice from friends and lovers, or seek refuge in material objects, yet we may still remain anxious and unfulfilled. Entertainments no longer give us much satisfaction, and we cannot find anything of beauty that does not somehow disappoint us; love is elusive, and nothing at all seems very meaningful or worthwhile. We simply flounder in our problems, looking for some method or technique that will relieve the tension and pressure of our insecurity and fear. In the end we may just privately cry.

There are rocks in the ocean that have been covered with water for thousands of years, yet, inside they remain dry. Similarly, we may try to understand ourselves by immersing ourselves in various ideas and philosophies, but if our hearts are closed and cold, real meaning does not truly touch us. No matter where we are or what we are doing, if we are not open, no one, not even the greatest teacher, can reach us.

Although we are adults, there is something of the infant within each of us. That child wants to grow, to dance, to mature, but he lacks the proper nourishment. The only way he knows how to find satisfaction is through demanding and grasping. So the ego stands behind each action—directing, manipulating, and possessing.

Occasionally we experience relief from our discontent, but soon our memories create new cravings. We try to repeat our past experiences, seeking new ways to please or be pleased, to satisfy or be satisfied; yet much of the time life still seems frustrating and hopeless. Although all of us desire happiness, few of us reach that goal because of the seemingly endless cycle of expectation and disappointment. But this cycle can end. If we can give up our attachment and grasping, it *is* possible to grow spiritually and to find genuine enjoyment. Bees feed on the nectar of flowers; they do not cling to the blossoms.

There is, then, a way—one that does not involve the ego. We can just be. We can forget the ego—toss it away—and completely relax. We do not need to think about 'me' or 'you' or what we are gaining or losing; we can just expand our feelings, our relaxation, our calmness, and our joy. We can keep expanding our awareness—free from ego, free from expectations, judgments, and identifications. When we do this we truly begin to grow.

Once we clearly recognize that our expectations lead only to disappointment and frustration, constant grasping no longer binds us, and we become more open to our experiences. We can find satisfaction anywhere—a simple walk may give more pleasure than any other entertainment. But until we open our hearts, there is little inspiration, inner light, or warmth to sustain us, for we are constantly undermining ourselves. Ultimately no one can help us very much unless we take the first step, listen to ourselves, encourage ourselves, and give ourselves confidence by taking refuge in our hearts.

So begin by listening to your heart, to your feelings and thoughts and to your inner dialogue. Pay close attention to everything that is happening within you. At first you may be judgmental—rejecting your immediate experience because of deep resentment for yourself or others. Or perhaps you feel dull and cold; your heart may be tight, and you may have difficulty feeling anything at all. But very gently and skillfully listen to your feelings. This is important. Listen to your heart—literally, listen to the beating of your heart. Usually we are not even aware of how fast or slow our hearts are beating. But rather than distracting yourself with thoughts and concepts, listen to your inner voice, and you will find yourself becoming much more relaxed and joyful.

When you listen very carefully, sometimes you can even hear a sound within the silence. This is not the rushing sound that you sometimes hear when your body is going through the natural process of releasing tension, but is the sound of your thoughts speaking. When your senses are very quiet and you are relaxed and concentrating, then it is possible to hear different tones. Sometimes you can hear a high, shrill tone or a deep voice— but this depends very much on your individual experience. There are actually ten different tones, each tone having a specific vibration. But to experience these, you must first develop your concentration and awareness until you are completely attentive and open.

It is important not to strive to attain any particular experience—so relax without distraction and without losing awareness. Occasionally, after an extended period of meditation, if you are very silent and alert, you may hear a beautiful, soft music in your body—a sort of silent music between the thoughts. Through meditation and your own sensitivity you can contact this silent inner music.

Before we can listen to the higher self within, we need to learn to accept and love ourselves. In time the heart center opens naturally and this is the beginning of the path of openness, compassion, and commitment. When the various body centers are opened, we can discover certain mental and physical signs or energies that affect both the emotions and the nervous system. We can actually feel how open the heart is, and how well we are communicating with it.

Once our hearts are open, all existence appears naturally beautiful and harmonious. This is not just another fantasy—it *is* possible to see or feel this way, and this is the essence of the spiritual teachings. The heart reveals all knowledge to us. Why the heart and not the mind? Because our egos control our heads, and our hearts are much more free.

When our hearts are open, no problem is too great. Even if we lose our possessions and our friends and are left alone with no one to support or guide us, we can find sustenance in our deepest feelings, in our inner silence. By utilizing our inner resources we can cope more easily with emotional and intellectual situations because we are no longer involved in the drama around us. Even if we have to face death, we can remain peaceful, calm, and balanced.

So we need to encourage our warm and positive feelings. This warmth is not a superficial or sentimental emotion—the kind that leads to imbalance and often creates 'panic' instead of calm. It is a genuine openness which is felt as a deep warmth in the center of the heart, which is our inner sanctuary, our own home.

It is in the heart center that our inner nature grows to fullness. Once the heart center opens, all blockages dissolve, and a spirit or intuition spreads throughout our entire body so that our whole being comes alive. This 'spirit' is sometimes spoken of as the essence of human energy or the essence of truth. But whatever it is called, unless we allow it to pervade us, our bodies may be active but our hearts remain closed. We are strangers to ourselves.

When we are able to integrate our minds with our hearts and our actions with our intuitions we can find genuine meaning in our lives. Our emotional difficulties and problems automatically diminish and we discover inspiration, insight, motivation, and strength. We become naturally self-nourishing, self-motivating, and self-confident. So, let us look at what is happening in our hearts. This is an essential preparation for experiencing the truth of our own lives.

Awakening Compassion

Like the sun which emits countless rays,
compassion is the source of all
inner growth and positive action.

Soon after we are born we become very familiar with our own suffering and confusion. Yet even after many years, we find ourselves still unaware of other people's sufferings. And our ability to communicate, even with those closest to us, is limited. We find it difficult to understand them, and often they find it difficult to understand us. Although we live in close proximity to hundreds, or even thousands of people with whom we share so many basic human problems, still we do not show much concern for one another.

Many of us, however, are looking for ways to understand and satisfy ourselves and others. But usually what we find is just collected information—concepts and theories having little to do with concerns of human development and understanding. Yet we study such information and think we have discovered real knowledge. If what we learn helps us to grow and progress inwardly, this may be true. But if it does not, year after year we can find ourselves in the same dull situations, following the same dull patterns, wasting our lives collecting information that has little real benefit for anyone. So, it is important *now* to closely observe our lives and learn to benefit from the knowledge and understanding which is within ourselves.

If we look honestly at ourselves what do we see? On the surface our lives may seem happy and comfortable, yet we may not be genuinely satisfied. Although we smile and act as if nothing were bothering us, we may be suffering, with no one to help us or to guide us properly. Protective of our position or self-image, we perpetuate our isolation and create our own little shell in a completely private world which no one else is allowed to enter. There we experience all our joy, as well as our failures and frustrations. There we can make all the mistakes we want and no one will ever know; there we conceal secret resentments and intolerant thoughts . . . forgetting that all such attitudes are like poison and will only produce further frustration and negativity.

So, on the one hand, we feel we need relationships with other people to bring us joy and friendship. But on the other hand, we set up a wall to protect ourselves from involvement and conflict, so that we seldom touch, trust, or truly share with each other. When we were younger, perhaps we tried to be more open with our feelings, but we were hurt and did not continue. Our egos were too vulnerable or our sympathy for others was not great enough, so eventually we became very isolated. And even now, we may have close friends or family, but if we are honest with ourselves, we see how lonely we are. We seldom open ourselves to anyone; and even when we do care for someone, often our caring comes from a sense of duty or from selfish expectations of reciprocation.

But, whatever our pretense, we can learn to care for this frightened and lonely person we may be. Caring for ourselves can be a tremendous source of protection against suffering and frustration. Self-confidence can help us apply our intelligence and knowledge to make our lives more balanced and harmonious. Through self-nurturing and development, we establish a friendship with ourselves; our hearts then open naturally, and compassion arises from within. As self-confidence and self-healing begin to develop, we start to show real kindness to ourselves and others.

Taking care of ourselves is not just another selfish act with a spiritual label. It is possible to give ourselves real warmth and sustenance without being motivated by self-love, because grasping for satisfaction is very different from learning to care for ourselves. Without compassion, thoughts and actions are based on desire for egotistical or selfish gratification. But genuine compassion, which is the antidote to ego, arises from a humble and fearless attitude of openness and generosity.

C ompassion is the bridge, the spiritual foundation for peace, harmony, and balance. The ego is the obstacle . . . playing games, grasping, being clever and ingenious; it essentially runs our lives. The ego has so programmed us physically and mentally that only compassion can break the ego's hold on us and enable us to develop our full potential as human beings.

Once we deeply experience our suffering and loneliness, we can imagine the many others in the world who experience the same feelings. We see that the conditions which give rise to such pain occur again and again, not only in this life but in many lifetimes; so we realize that we must try to alter this situation as soon as possible. Once we recognize all that we have in common with others, a feeling of compassion naturally arises and we no longer treat other people with such indifference. We more easily understand their problems, and as we learn how to heal ourselves, we begin to use our knowledge to help them as well.

Once we learn to care for ourselves we can learn to appreciate the preciousness and uniqueness of each individual. We welcome others warmly and joyfully into our hearts, for we no longer feel defensive. We easily see when others relate to *us* in this way—their eyes are alive and their faces are radiant.

Even though compassion has this opening power, often, we do not feel compassionate even toward our own parents. Perhaps, when we were children, our relationships with them were not open and warm, so now we may reject or even hate our own mothers who gave us birth. But concern for parents is basic to the psychological well-being of any civilization—parents care for their children, and children care for their parents. This relationship is very important; yet often there is great misunderstanding and resentment in families, which carries on for whole lifetimes.

We can begin to develop compassion for our parents by thinking how much they endured in order to protect and support us, how much they helped us even when their lives were difficult. Perhaps they could have exercised greater wisdom in raising us; possibly they were ignorant or caught by their own grasping minds and desires. But they did try their best according to their limited ability. So we can feel empathy toward them as though we were living *their* lives, had their parents, their childhood, education, and experiences. We can try to picture our infancy—twenty, thirty, forty years ago. We were tiny and weak, yet somehow we managed to mature. As we grew we went through many experiences and now we are adults and can do whatever we like. But it is valuable to remember our origins and how much pain, worry, and suffering our parents experienced in order to support us and give us the opportunity to grow. Once we look back and remember all this, our hearts become more open toward our parents.

Compassion is a healthy psychological attitude, because it does not involve expectations or demands. Even if we are not able to accomplish very much on a physical level, at least we can have the desire to be a loving person with a compassionate heart—the wish to help others, spontaneously, with no reservations. This attitude automatically opens our hearts and develops our compassion. Then we can sincerely say to ourselves, "If there is any way I can learn to increase my compassion or understanding of humanity, then I wish to receive that teaching—whatever it is, wherever it exists—and take the responsibility to use that knowledge to help others."

As we develop compassion we begin to sacrifice and surrender our hearts. We do not even care if the other person acknowledges our attitude or our actions—he may not even be aware of them. As we lessen self-grasping, we have a deepened feeling of fulfillment and satisfaction that can expand and give our lives great meaning. What else in human existence has such value?

We may be very intelligent and powerful, very cultured and well-traveled, but of what value is that? Only one night's dream, and it is gone. Every experience imaginable has the same impermanent nature; only compassion gives lasting happiness. Unlike the fleeting moments of 'happiness' we usually experience, the joy which arises from compassion is neither sentimental nor romantic. It is non-dual—with no discrimination between giver and receiver.

At least once a day it is helpful to think about the loneliness, confusion, suffering, and ignorance we all experience. This leads to the understanding of how all of these painful conditions—from birth to the present moment—came to be. Once we understand, we naturally become more relaxed and open. Our problems do not seem so serious, and we are able to enjoy life and even laugh at ourselves, because we understand and appreciate our lives for what they are.

Compassion is felt in the center of the heart, and the source of compassion is our feelings, our living experience. Until the positive energy of compassion flows through our hearts, we accomplish little of real value. We may simply be occupying our minds with hollow words and images. We may master various sciences or philosophies, but without compassion, we are just empty scholars trapped in vicious circles of craving, grasping, and anxiety. There is little real meaning or satisfaction in our lives. But when our energy is awakened, relationships with others become healthy and effortless—we have no feeling of duty or obligation, because whatever we do feels naturally and spontaneously 'right'. Like the sun which emits countless rays, compassion is the source of all inner growth and positive action.

So, at this time, when man has the power to completely destroy the earth, it is especially important to develop whatever is beautiful, beneficial, and meaningful

. . . and to practice compassion. In the beginning, our compassion is like a candle—gradually we need to develop compassion as radiant as the sun. When compassion is as close as our breath, as alive as our blood, then we will understand how to live and work in the world effectively and to be of help to both ourselves and others.

We begin by touching our own essential natures, and then we open ourselves to friends, parents, and family. Eventually, we expand this feeling and share it with every living being, extending this openness to all of nature . . . to mountains, water, wind, sun, and stars. When we feel open to all existence, our relationships naturally become harmonious. This compassion need not be manifested physically—it simply arises through accepting and expanding an open mental attitude. The power of compassion can totally transform both ourselves and others so that our lives become radiant and light.

So try to visualize all the beings in the world—particularly those who have problems or who are experiencing pain. Especially remember your parents and friends, whether they are still alive or not, and then all others. Free yourself from selfish motivations and transform your problems and emotions into deep compassion towards all beings and all things in nature, so that the entire universe is flooded with compassion. Let this compassion radiate outward from every part of your body, and let us together send our power and energy to all beings so that they may overcome their obstacles and become healthy and happy.

Part Two

RELAXATION

Expanding Feeling

*This feeling of expansion is much more powerful
than the physical sensation of joy—
it is deep, vast, infinite.*

We all have within us the resources to be healthy and balanced; it is simply a matter of directing and utilizing our energies properly. This 'direction', however, is not a matter of a forced or disciplined control. It is a natural process which begins to function when we learn to relax and utilize certain ways of breathing, feeling, and thinking that help us to adjust our inner balance and allow our energies to flow more freely.

Relaxation is a healing system which can be used to relieve our anxieties and frustrations—the pressures that so often cause our energies to stagnate, and thus prevent us from expanding our meditation and awareness. By deep relaxation we purify our inner energies. We can begin to relax by just becoming aware of whatever feelings we are experiencing—the tightness in our muscles, difficulties in breathing, or pressure in our heads. We need to be aware of, touch, and communicate with all the feelings that we experience in our daily lives. Then through the use of massage and certain exercises we can learn to loosen these physical and mental constrictions. When we learn to relax the body, breath, and mind, the body becomes healthy, the mind becomes clear, and our awareness becomes balanced.

Once we relax and our minds are free from distractions, we begin to feel more open and natural. This is the time to silence inner dialogue and conceptual thinking; once these are silenced, it is quite a simple matter to improve the quality of our meditation. Then, throughout the day, we can continue to nourish the feeling energy we have contacted, and thus continue to develop a watchful, positive awareness.

So sit back, breathe deeply about ten or fifteen times, and slowly and completely relax your whole body. Relax your eyes, and let your mouth fall open. Follow your breath down your arms, your legs. Completely let yourself go. Give yourself time, and sense your entire body from your toes to the top of your head. Can you feel your heart beat? Can you feel the pulse in your toes? Then, very gently and very slowly, massage your head, neck, chest, arms, legs, and feet—so that you feel a warm flow of energy in each cell. In this way, let your body relax completely.

In the beginning, it is helpful to concentrate on a particular area, such as the head. Most of the time our heads are busier than the rest of the body, and feelings tend to clog and constrict our necks, shoulders, and facial muscles—so begin by massaging your head and feel the energy move through your entire body. During the massage, it is best not to be concerned with whether the feeling is good or bad—just feel it. It is important for all of your muscles to be as loose as possible, so as you massage your body, ask yourself, "Is there any tightness, any muscle tension?" If so, pay particular attention to the tense areas until you gradually relax every part of your body. Then take the time to listen to your body in silence; wherever the energy is blocked or there is tenseness or pain, become loose and relaxed.

Now relax your breath so that your breathing is calm, and unself-conscious. Take a few deep breaths—inhale very slowly and deeply, then hold the breath for just a moment, completely silent, and then exhale very quietly and softly through your mouth and nose equally. Feel the energy circulate through your bloodstream and very gently watch your feelings. You do not need to concentrate on breathing—just let the feeling be, and let your consciousness experience that feeling. If you just ignore your breath it naturally becomes relaxed and still, and your body energy comes alive with very subtle, warm, sensitive feelings—like having the sun shine on your body.

When you are very quiet and relaxed, a warm sensation rises from within. The whole body is alert, and you feel almost empty, as if the body itself were gradually disappearing; the heaviness and solidity are no longer there, but just a very open, silent feeling of expanding vastness. There are no instructions to remember, no concentration—you are just a part of that vast openness. The quieter you become, the more energy you can feel. In this way, you can experience your body as open space, and live within that feeling. Expand that feeling energy as much as possible, without commenting on or interpreting it. When you exercise this expansion, space itself is exercising, perfectly balanced—like a precision drawing or a beautiful work of art.

As soon as you touch this inner feeling, you forget your body and your breath. You can actually *become* that feeling, and then you can expand it, as though you were just leaving the womb . . . this feeling can be almost unlimited. Later on, nothing else may seem to exist —only this feeling experience. You can exist fully within the energy, so that wherever the feeling leads, you just follow it . . . further and further, like the ripples from a single stone spreading outward until they cover the entire surface of the lake. In this way, you become completely silent—your cells, your energy, your breath, and your awareness.

Finally, relax your mind. Usually, because our inner dialogues are constantly projecting interpretations, concepts, and judgments, the mind is very restless and nervous. Watch these movements of your mind, without following any particular thought or performing any specific action. Do not try to concentrate too hard. Awareness is already there, but it does not stay in any particular place; awareness does not cling to any 'thing'. So just experience the immediate feeling—a sort of 'feeling energy'. When you do not grasp at judgments or thoughts, you can experience the feeling as a part of your mental activity, like swimming in the middle of the ocean; there will be nothing in your consciousness except total feeling.

In the beginning, you may think you are only imagining this energy, but the more familiar with it you become, the more you can direct it. After a time you will experience it as a kind of heat or warmth—finally as a feeling of deep love and joy. This energy refreshes your consciousness and changes your thought patterns. Your thinking becomes increasingly balanced, and energy rises and circulates more freely throughout your entire system.

You can expand this relaxation even within thought. Try to hold one single thought, and then expand it; reach the inside of that thought. Expand it and enlarge it . . . without judging or labeling it . . . without holding it as subject or object. The feeling or energy will still remain, but without discrimination or conceptual limitations. Once you have touched or experienced this deeper feeling, you can then bring the feeling into every thought and experience.

In this way we can learn how to expand awareness. First, on the physical level, through massage and physical exercises; second, on the mental level, through breathing and experiencing these feelings more deeply; and third, on the level of subtle awareness, through direct experience. When we taste that feeling, we find that the feeling itself has become infinite!

Thus, whenever we have a good feeling, we should expand it; the quality of that feeling should not be lost, for joy, love, and beauty are very satisfying and fulfilling. For example, we have beautiful feelings when we think about making love; if we expand that feeling and touch it deeply, then it will last a longer time. Usually when we feel happy and joyful, and experience pleasant sensations, we try to preserve the feeling by grasping the thought. Yet this greater, expanded feeling is much vaster than thought, and thus we limit it by trying to encompass it by thoughts.

In the beginning physical contact—as through massage—is important, but later on the physical body becomes almost symbolic, for the feeling experience continues to expand beyond the body. If we can retain that experience, then we know that it is not just imagination—the experience is actually happening! This is a more subtle level of higher awareness which has an ecstatic quality—there is not that much feeling, only awareness. Later on we can integrate that feeling or awareness within the physical body. But again, the feeling experience is not just physical—it becomes a totally encompassing experience. Once the body is very quiet and restful, we can discover experiences and understandings that we could hardly have conceived of before . . . without words, without concepts . . . similar to pure knowledge.

On this higher level of awareness, beautiful feelings, like an inner massage, duplicate themselves spontaneously, like ocean waves rising and falling. When we find this place in our practice, we can exercise and stretch this feeling. This feeling of expansion is much more powerful than the physical sensation of joy—it is deep, vast, infinite. Our bodies and breath may feel very small, but our minds experience—without words or concepts— many different tones and qualities, beautiful images, and even deeper subtleties. The first kind of joy which arises is innocent, like a child's joy. It expands to feelings of happiness, then various physical and mental sensations arise, and later it becomes almost overwhelming.

As we develop this beautiful, balanced experience, we may find that it is quite close to what is sometimes called 'mystic experience'. It is difficult to tell whether this energy is 'physical' or 'mental', but all living organisms share this characteristic patterning—this pure energy. It is always there, even though we commonly do not know how to contact it. Often we need certain conditions—a quiet place, a light diet, or psychological exercises—to contact this energy. But once we taste this experience and *feel* it directly, we can bring that memory back into awareness and find that pure energy, or pure knowledge, everywhere.

Body, Breath, and Mind

*In order to develop higher awareness, we
need to integrate the body, breath, and mind.*

Generally, we think of the body as only a physical entity made up of skin, bones, muscles, and internal organs; but these are themselves broken down successively into cells, molecules, and atoms. As we investigate the nature of the atom we find certain forces that hold the atom together. When we consider the body itself more closely, we can observe similar elusive forces or energy patterns.

Within the body, on a very fine, subtle level, each cell or atom has a kind of nuclear energy which is identical with the energy in the field outside the body. Relatively speaking, we cannot say that the body is like 'space', because our physical structure seems quite solid. But in the ultimate sense, the space *outside* the body and the space that the body *occupies* are not separate. This total space forms a natural unity, like water flowing into water.

At certain times when we are very relaxed, positive energies increase so that we can actually 'feel' internal and external space become one, as though our bodies were dropping away . . . we lose the impression of solidity. The resultant feeling of oneness is very important, because when our bodies are completely loose and relaxed, the energy within our cells begins to flow smoothly and naturally throughout our whole system, without any manipulation or extra effort on our part. This energy manifests as balance, joy, or even love.

In developing relaxation, we can concentrate on a particular feeling such as physical calmness—then gradually expand that feeling so that it extends outward and inward, beyond the physical body. We can concentrate on our body stillness alone or on our breath alone, or on the silencing of our thoughts. And as we expand this feeling of inner silence, we can feel the energy circulate through and beyond our physical bodies.

This energy has three elements which together form the basic 'pattern' of our lives. Our attitudes and actions depend on how well these three are balanced; our health, happiness, and even the length of our lives, also depend on this balance.

The first element is the physical structure or 'body pattern' though which energy flows. The second we call 'breath'—but it is not just breath. It has a quality of motility; it is a moving, flowing sort of energy. The third element is the 'subtle body energy', which is more elusive than breath. All three elements are inseparably linked to and cannot function without each other; yet each has its own specific characteristics and qualities. Together they create the basic structure of the physical body, combining in a complex, mysterious manner to create what we call life. In some ways they can be equated with the body, breath, and mind; but they are much more than what we usually understand by these terms.

The 'body pattern', the physical structure through which energy flows, is more than just a 'body'. The mental energy of our attitudes and actions creates a certain 'atmosphere' which accumulates around us on levels beyond our physical substance—this is sometimes called the 'subtle' or 'etheric' body. Even though it cannot ordinarily be seen, it is always a part of us. We can liken the 'subtle' body to the upper atmosphere of the earth, which is a continuation of the lower atmosphere, but is made up of different elements and has a different quality.

'Breath' is much more than our usual concept of breathing; it is connected with other energy flows, and its quality changes depending on our emotional states. When we breathe too shallowly or too heavily, this affects the rest of our system; when we balance our breath—by balancing our emotions—the body and mind become balanced as well. Breath is like a bridge connecting body and mind.

The 'subtle body energy' can be equated with mind, but not with mind as we know it. Usually the mind formulates experience into thoughts and concepts, into subject and object. But there is another way of experiencing which does not create this dualism. When the mind is balanced, there is no time, no consciousness, no awareness *of*; there is just a very special energy that is always present.

The 'body pattern', 'breath', and the 'subtle body energy', interconnect with the four centers of the body—the head, throat, heart, and navel. 'Body' is connected with the navel center, 'breath' with the throat center, and 'mind' with the head center. Body, breath and mind all come together and are integrated in the heart.

Each of the body centers functions on many levels. During times when our hearts are open and our minds are not simply involved in an intellectual process, our energy moves to the deeper levels and gradually into intrinsic awareness—into an equilibrium state that is one of the highest of human experiences. This awareness is felt in the heart, as well as in the mind.

Each center of the body is capable of vibrating with positive energy, such as kindness, love, and compassion. Each center is also capable of a very depressing and confusing restlessness or dullness.

When the three elements or energies move through the centers, certain conditions or attitudes are produced —physical sicknesses, mental blockages, emotional troubles . . . or feelings of lightness, radiance, and total openness. The basic patterns of our physical functioning both determine and are determined by how the energy flows through these very subtle centers. Whenever we are sick, unbalanced, or have negative feelings, these are always indicated by the *pattern*, the *movement*, and the *essence* of energy within the body. Therefore, in order to be healthy we should learn how to balance our body, breath, and mind.

We may balance and help to heal ourselves by concentrating on various parts of our bodies. These concentration practices are simple, but quite specific. When our bodies are not balanced or our physical energy is being blocked, when we are sick or afraid, it is helpful to concentrate on the stomach, at a point below the navel.

If we are feeling lonely—cut off from other people, or if we wish to develop compassion or joy we can concentrate on the heart center. In order to develop emotional balance or to overcome nervousness, cravings, or dissatisfactions, we need to concentrate on the throat center. And, since the centers are interrelated, the more we concentrate on the throat, the more the heart becomes balanced.

When our mental awareness or our consciousness is not strong or well-focused, when we feel dreamy, lost, or caught by our dualistic minds, we need to concentrate on the crown of the head or the point on the forehead between the eyes. If we wish to develop generosity or a lucid mind, it is helpful to concentrate on the head center.

Since body, breath, and mind all become balanced at the heart center, it is there that we need to develop more openness. Basically, if the heart center becomes more open, it is very easy for the body and mind to function well together and to support and appreciate each other.

When we focus on specific areas of the body, we can examine the different feelings or tones which arise, and we can see which area is the strongest and which is the weakest. This will help us determine how to work with our energy. For example, when one area is very tight or constricted, we can focus our energy there, and try to relax and loosen the tension. Or if another area is either particularly active or very dull, we can work to bring energy away from or toward that area. We can work with this energy in many ways, but this should give an idea of what is involved.

At various times physical exercises may be helpful in balancing and re-vitalizing the body, breath, and mind; but if these exercises are done merely mechanically, or if we become fascinated with one particular method, our openness and growth can be endangered by a narrowing of opportunities and perspective. Furthermore, not every technique is appropriate for everyone, so it is important to have proper guidance in selecting which methods are best to practice and for how long.

These practices and exercises are useful for integrating ourselves and developing higher awareness. They help to release a flow of energy through our bodies; this energy enriches our senses, calms our restless minds, and brings us peace and balance.

Healing
Through Positive Energy

When positive or joyous feelings and attitudes
pass through each organ and circulate throughout our whole system,
our physical and chemical energies are transformed and balanced.

O ur bodies and minds are constantly interacting:
Most of what comes into the mind enters through
the senses—and most of our feelings, although experienced physically, are interpreted mentally. When this
interrelationship of body and mind is not balanced and
feelings do not flow smoothly through the body, tension
builds up, giving rise to negative emotions which can
cause both physical and mental illness.

In order to develop and maintain health and balance, it is important to treat the body and mind as an
integrated system. To do this it is helpful to carefully
observe their interrelationship and to learn how this
interrelationship works.

Mind is related to the senses, which are related to the
body, while the body is related to the world. Each one
leads to the other. Each has its own pattern, and together
they all act and interact very quickly, but each process
also follows specific channels. As the senses communicate information to the mind, the mind begins to make

decisions, which involve judgments, concepts, and dualities, that then create separateness and conflict. Therefore, as soon as this process begins, conflict is automatically initiated—conflict within the mind itself, conflict between body and mind, conflict between the senses and the mind . . . first internally, then externally.

Certain feelings are stronger in some areas of the body than in others, and vary in intensity at different times—so in the beginning it is important to pinpoint the *area* and the *intensity* of the feeling. Usually, however, feelings accumulate like dust and become so mixed together that we cannot separate them. Feelings can be either positive, negative, or neutral, and sometimes feelings can arise without any apparent rational cause. These are like hidden residues that have long been accumulating in the physical body; we cannot predict when they will erupt.

When our awareness is undeveloped, our senses often do not even register the impressions received—the impressions just float away like letters drawn on moving water. We can, however, consciously develop our sensitivity—which will cause our awareness to improve as well. For example, when we are skilled we can see in another's eyes whether or not he or she is mentally and physically balanced.

We should begin, however, by carefully observing our own thoughts and feelings. When we watch our minds, we can observe an almost unlimited flow of images and concepts, and this flow, in itself, indicates a negative, unbalanced state. For whenever we are involved in categorizing or interpreting, the mind cuts itself off from the experience, causing us to become caught in an endless progression of thoughts. As soon as one thought or image arises, it leads to another, which may be interpreted or associated with still another; and this chain is very difficult to break. So our minds become caught in continual motion, and are given no chance to rest and replenish their energy. The result is that our bodies and minds become exhausted, and mental agitations accumulate.

If we observe this process closely, we see that when our senses initially perceive an object, the first tendency is to grasp the object. This leads to further craving and attachment, which cause us to become fixed in certain patterns of behavior. Each time the mind moves toward an object, we lose energy—although this is sometimes difficult to perceive, because the degree of loss depends on the intensity of the situation. When the depletion of energy becomes too great, we lose our balance, and negative emotions, which can affect both our feelings and perceptions, then easily arise. For instance, when we are sad or depressed, and hear beautiful music, we often cannot appreciate it; when we are offered delicious food, we cannot enjoy it.

There are times when the stress from our worries and fears, our memories and fantasies, constricts our energy to the point where we even harm our own bodies or minds. We can become so out of touch with ourselves, that our bodies are not aware of our minds, and our minds are not aware of our bodies. So, although our mental and physical difficulties are actually caused by an imbalance in our systems, we tend to blame our difficulties on outside influences. We suppress or reject our symptoms, and thus we treat ourselves as objects, or as our own enemies.

Once we learn to relax and develop a positive attitude, we can break through this state of inner stagnation, so that the energy is free to flow naturally and harmoniously. In the Himalayas, porters carry over a hundred pounds of weight—day and night—up and down mountains. When the baggage is finally lifted from their backs, their step becomes light and easy. Similarly, when we develop positive energy, the resulting inner awareness relieves our psychological burden; and we begin to feel light and joyful. When we learn to calm and integrate the body, breath, and mind, our whole system becomes vitalized and healthy.

The self-healing process needs a strong foundation built of relaxation, joy, love, and compassion. We need to relax the body, balance the emotions, and divert our energy from negative to positive thinking. Then we can begin to loosen our mental and physical constraints—our anxiety, tension, worry, and fear. As we become more open, we experience a sense of liberation and the energy is free to flow within us. There are more specific methods we can use for healing, such as concentration, mantra, visualization, and various physical and mental exercises; but the basic process is to relax and balance our energy.

When you are in a very emotional or highly excitable state, sit down and breathe softly and gently. Do not pay attention to your emotions, but just follow your breath and its rhythm. Following the sensation of your breath as it flows through your body can help you calm and heal both your body and mind.

When you have a physical or emotional blockage, reflect upon a joyful memory or visualize a beautiful garden; imagine whatever pleases you and makes you happy. As you do this, your mind and body will naturally slow down and relax. Through relaxation you can begin to sort out and work with your feelings and emotions, and watch them rise and fall like waves on the ocean. Your tension and tightness will loosen, and you will become calm and peaceful.

These two simple relaxation practices can help to integrate your body, mind, and senses, so that they function together harmoniously. This integration of the body and mind is essential for health and happiness.

Therefore, like a dike which must be built in the dry season in order to give protection during the time of floods, we must prepare our awareness sufficiently so that we will not be swept away when our emotions arise. Then once we calm our emotions and anxieties, we can leave behind unnecessary or artificial patterns of behavior and relate more directly to our immediate experience; thus we can become grounded. What is truly valuable for our lives becomes clear; our confusion lessens and our life-patterns become more wholesome and purposeful. Once we learn to calm our minds, mental and physical vitality, as well as health and balance, become possible.

These days, however, most of us depend on external or artificial means to keep healthy and free from pain. But when we bring ourselves back into balance so that the energy is flowing smoothly, our bodies and minds have the resources to protect themselves. The cure for sickness is within us—for the natural state is balance.

We ourselves are the remedy to restore this inner balance, because our whole body is in essence one universe. Chemically, our entire system is naturally self sufficient—we can open ourselves to positive energies and channel them throughout the body. Whatever we need is uniquely there—the prescription is there; the remedy is there. As we develop these positive energies, they refine and transform our bodies into healthy, clear, and open channels. Then whether positive or negative experiences happen, we can remain balanced.

Through the process of developing these energies, the levels of our experience transcend the physical plane; eventually we can even experience mind and matter as one. This realization is very similar in character to infinity, because pure energy is experienced everywhere.

These levels are always present, and, like close friends, are always accessible to us. Realizing this, we can constructively use every situation which arises, and our tendency to get caught in negative emotions decreases. We begin to live without grasping, craving, or attachment—and thus do not develop further binding patterns. Positive energy, itself, becomes a cure, and a self-healing process naturally takes place. The physical blockages which cause many psycho-somatic problems begin to dissolve, and when the body becomes healthy, refreshed, and cleansed of poisons, the mind also becomes clear and lucent.

We learn to utilize and benefit from our energy by living within our present experience. Once we have control of the subtle energy, we can distribute it to the physical body, the emotional body, and the psychic body. By stimulating and directing positive, joyous feelings we can change the essence of our inner patterns and experience. When positive or joyous feelings and attitudes pass through each organ and circulate throughout our whole system, our physical and chemical energies are transformed and balanced. In other words, *we have the opportunity to recreate our bodies through positive energy.*

Part Three

MEDITATION

Unfolding Meditation

As we experience this deeper level
of meditation, we will find that
the nature of mind is meditation,
and that, itself, is actually
the enlightened experience.

Almost all spiritual disciplines practice some form of meditation. Ordinarily, meditation is viewed as a form of thinking used in combination with words, images, or concepts. But meditation is not thinking *about* something. The meditative experience may seem subjective—*my* consciousness, *my* awareness. But as we look further into the meditative state, we find that awareness is neither subjective nor objective; it also cannot be conceptually analyzed. Awareness is a natural openness that takes place when the mind is left to function freely on its own—with no interruptions, distractions, or expectations.

Meditative awareness is like completely open space. But not space as we commonly understand it, because awareness is not a place, nor does it have any particular form or shape. This space is neither outside the body nor inside the mind. It is not mental or physical, and yet, at the same time, it is a deep, integrated sense of stillness, openness, and balance—which is the experience of meditation itself.

Traditionally, beginning meditation involves certain practices, such as intense concentration, the visualization of various images, or the chanting of mantras. Teachers emphasize different practices depending on the needs of the student. For instance, a teacher may tell one student to go alone to a quiet place and be completely silent for half an hour or forty-five minutes, and he may tell another to go to the mountains or ocean and chant very loudly. Someone else may be instructed to gaze at the sky and just be open. Others may be given devotional or ritual practices.

Generally, however, our practice should be whatever calms and relaxes us—whatever works best for the development of stillness and concentration. Meditation helps us to be calm and happy . . . to enjoy life, to be cheerful, and to deal effectively with both our physical and mental problems. Our lives become balanced when we are able to integrate whatever we experience with our meditation. We can include our joy and happiness, as well as our anger, resentment, frustration, and unhappiness . . . all the emotions that we feel throughout the day. We can turn all our emotions into the relaxation and calmness of meditation.

In the beginning, meditation seems simple—to be quiet, still, calm, and relaxed, and perhaps to follow specific instructions. But gradually, as we refine our meditation, we realize that meditation involves much more than just relaxing and dealing with our thoughts and emotions. Meditation is actually a process of seeking truth or understanding, of trying to discover the nature of existence and of the human mind. To discover such knowledge we have to go very deeply into meditation, and find out who we really are.

So simply, how do you meditate? First of all, the body must be very still, very quiet. Physically relax your muscles and let go of all your tension. Then sit in a comfortable position and stay completely still, not moving at all. Breathe very softly and gently . . . inhale and exhale slowly and smoothly. As much as you can, completely relax so that your entire nervous system becomes calm. Then quiet the mind; still your thoughts through inner silence. There are various ways to do this, but as too many instructions may be distracting, just very naturally relax your body, breath, and mind. The body becomes still, the breath balanced, and the mind and senses very peaceful. At this time you deeply feel and enjoy your senses coming alive. You can see that meditation is not a difficult task or something foreign or imported—it is a part of your nature.

There is no need to try to accomplish some goal, since trying itself becomes an obstacle to relaxation. Pushing yourself too hard, or attempting to follow a rigid set of instructions, may cause problems—for when you exert too much effort, you can find yourself caught between getting something and not getting it, making internal reports to yourself while trying to be silent. When you try to conceptually experience the 'perfect meditation', you may end up creating endless internal conflicts or inner dialogues.

Because concepts are necessary in introducing meditation, from the beginning, the meditator is separated from the experience. But when you become involved in the actual practice of meditation, you find that meditation goes far beyond conceptualization. If you continue to relax and calm your mind, eventually no effort at all will be needed for your meditation.

When you are just learning to meditate, it is best to experience yourself totally, without rejecting or exclud-

ing any part of yourself. All of your thoughts and feelings can be a part of your meditation—you can taste each one, then gradually move on. In this way, you can begin to discover the various subtle layers and states of the mind. The mind simply observes its own natural process; every thought, desire, and motivation is a natural aid to this basic type of meditation. On the relative level, there are still distinctions of good and bad, but when you realize a meditative state, you no longer perceive relative discriminations as accurately defining experience. Meditation transcends dualism. Whatever you experience can be seen as perfect, for the quality of perfection lies within your mind, not in anything external.

When memories or discomforts arise, you may feel a little uneasy, but this feeling will pass if you do not mentally hold on to any thought in particular. Just remain very loose and quiet and do not think 'about' meditation. Simply accept yourself. You are not trying to *learn* meditation; you *are* the meditation. Your entire body, breath, thoughts, senses, and awareness—your total being—are all part of the meditation. You do not have to worry about losing it. Your entire energy-field is a part of the meditation, so you do not need to follow any specific instructions or worry about achieving a particular experience.

A famous Tibetan lama once said of meditation, "The best water is rocky water." As water flows over rocks, its quality improves and is purified. So the best meditation is one that is flowing and free—with nothing to hold on to—for once we hold a position, we are brought to a standstill by our grasping. How much more beautiful is the freedom to flow to the higher meditative states! When another master was asked, "When you are concentrating, where is your concentration?" he answered that there was no subject, no position, no goal.

As we experience this deeper level of meditation, we find that the nature of mind *is* meditation. And this, itself, is actually the enlightened experience. This experience is free from everything, and yet at the same time, it manifests all and everything. This, itself, is liberation.

Observing Thoughts

Within the immediate, direct, and
present moment of the experience, there is
nothing you can say or think or label.

Some meditations involve analysis, while others focus directly on immediate experience—each type
opens up different areas of awareness. Analytical meditation is especially useful for developing concentration
and awareness. However, analytical understanding and
mental preparation can only take us up to a certain point,
because at a deeper level the idea itself stops. Ideas cannot function without the words and concepts that are
themselves part of the rational mind; when the 'idea'
stops, all that is left is a kind of immediate certainty that
is based on experiential realization. In letting go of the
intellectual, rational mind, we contact a deeper, more
subtle energy which we experience directly.

Some meditators can immediately transcend thoughts
and emotions, and go directly into the experience of
meditative awareness. But for others it is helpful to first
analyze what is involved: what the relationship is between the meditator and the meditation, how the relationship is established, who is watching, who is inter-

preting the experience. The sharper this analysis is and the more deeply we investigate, the more quickly we can become open to the meditative experience. Every question asked widens the vision and decreases doubts, questions, or problems. Then once this analysis stops, meditation very naturally becomes spontaneous, immediate, direct.

A very good beginning exercise in analytical meditation is to count how many thoughts you have in one hour. Write them down and categorize them into positive, negative, or neutral. Simply observe how many thoughts pass through your head in one hour, and continue to do this every day for at least one week.

Then pick out one specific thought, and, holding it as long as you can, think about it. This can be any thought you may have, whether negative or positive. Hold it as long as you can; do not let it go. In other words, there should be no second thought—just concentrate on the one single thought. Do not try to judge it, locate it, or see how it is, but just let it *be*. When that thought is finished, and another comes, again try to do the same thing . . . and again and again try to see how long you can hold one thought. Do this four or five times during the day.

After you do this exercise, examine your relationship to the observer within, that is, to the one who is observing or recognizing your thoughts, concepts, and feelings. Who is watching? You may say your 'awareness' or 'intuition' is watching, your 'consciousness' or 'subjective mind', or the person that you refer to as 'me' or 'I' or 'ego' or 'self'. But how is this 'I' related to the thought, and how do they work together? What are the differences and conflicts between that 'me' and that 'mind'?

Instead of examining these things analytically, try now to examine them experientially. The more you observe your own experience, the more you will discover direct answers to these questions. But when you do not observe the thought carefully, you may find yourself labeling or judging the experience. When this happens you will not be contacting the deeper, more subtle levels of the experience, and your answers then will be somewhat superficial.

'I' am the 'subject', which means that 'I' perceive and experience images, feelings, ideas, memories. How are that 'I' and that 'experience' connected to each other? If they are the same, then how does the 'I' see them or experience them? If they are different, what are the differences between them? Once the 'I' has a specific 'experience', is it interpreted directly—without words or imagery—or is it labeled and judged?

Within the immediate moment of the experience, there is nothing you can say or think or label. There is nothing tangible to put into words and concepts—experience is not even there! What you may discover is that the experience itself dissolves, and all your problems with it . . . and this becomes meditation. In other words, after all the inner words, thoughts, and relationships dissolve, you just remain in the experience—without the experiencer—as long as you like.

Do not formulate any specific idea of how this 'experience' should be; do not even think that you are meditating or having an experience. Just allow the experience to be, without worrying about what is happening or how it happened; there is no need to report the experience back to your self, since there is no longer any self remaining. If any specific word or image or concept arises and you think, "That's good," or "Now I see," or "Now I understand this clearly," then you need to examine the thought again, until you have nothing to say, interpret, or explain.

Even good meditators may have spent many years meditating before freeing their minds from the ceaseless progression of thoughts. So we can save a lot of valuable time, by receiving precise instructions, and learning to meditate properly. For example, without detailed knowledge of atomic power, we can attempt for hundreds of years to produce an explosion. But when we have accurate knowledge of atomic energy, we may have no trouble in quickly being able to produce a nuclear reaction.

The secret 'formula' or 'path' that leads to higher meditation is not to identify, not to take a position, not to hold onto anything within the meditation. When we know how to enter meditation directly, we can quickly transcend ordinary discursive thought, and with proper guidance, we can transmute many lifetimes of negative karma in a very short time. This 'secret' knowledge of meditation becomes a self-sustaining source of inspiration. We become simply *centerless*, with no subject, no object, and nothing in between—nothing to upset our being poised.

Meditation transcends time, the senses, and subject-object relationships. By transcending these three, meditation takes us beyond the intellectual or rational level of consciousness. It is like looking through a screen; on one side of consciousness is all existence—thoughts, emotions, negativity, and our life patterns; on the other side is a very fine energy level—a deep meditative state.

Transforming Anxiety

*By utilizing the penetrative quality
of direct awareness we can become sensitive
to our emotions before they arise
and thus begin to break our habit patterns
and our attachment to them.*

Awareness is always accessible within ourselves, within our energy. But when we are distracted or emotionally entangled, we may have no idea what is actually happening in ourselves. Everything may seem very dream-like, and we may find ourselves going from one conversation or activity to another, moody and anxious, or possibly with a false sense of spontaneity and freedom. At other times we find ourselves thinking continually about the past or the future, or struggling with current 'problems'—inadequacies, hesitations, self-deceptions, fears, infatuations, and guilts—our energies so caught up in a variety of emotional entanglements that we feel confused, worn out, tense, and anxious. By working with these emotions in our meditation, we can learn to free ourselves from their influence.

Emotions may not have eyes, mouths or stomachs, but they can still suck our energies, hypnotize us, and destroy our natural state of balance. Emotions have the power to lure us into an artificial realm of sensation that is able to gain control of our positive energies. People seem to *need* emotions, like they need salt for food. But emotions are dangerous and unstable, for what begins as pleasure, often ends up as pain. And when we are in the midst of an emotional situation, we can be blinded by the dynamics of the situation so that our perceptions and perspectives are no longer clear.

One of the most difficult emotions to handle is anxiety. On the surface anxiety may not seem that great a problem, but as far as our human consciousness is concerned, it can disturb our meditative openness to the point where we completely lose our balance. We let positive opportunities slip away through loss of awareness; anxiety pushes and divides us, creating separateness, confusion, and dissatisfaction. And when we are not mindful of our anxiety it becomes increasingly hard to control.

Needing can be very demanding. We continually feel the need for what can satisfy *me* . . . my ego, my mind, my feelings, my senses. Our lack of confidence causes us to feel a need for support or stimulation—by friends, intellectual perceptions, or material objects. When we do not receive this contact, we can sometimes feel so alone and without support, that anxiety drains all the energy from our bodies. Once our energy is gone, we feel empty, depressed, and even despairing.

It seems that the only way we know how to search for satisfaction or self-fulfillment is through endless craving. Although we sometimes manage to temporarily satisfy our desires, the satisfaction usually lasts only a short time, and we are left with disappointment that leads to even more anxiety. Most human beings run on anxiety. Craving and grasping are like a candle, and anxiety is the flame. One word for this continual frustration is *samsara*, which means that we are dissatisfied and unhappy because we can seldom get what we want. We are continually seeking—moving toward what is outside ourselves.

When we lack confidence in ourselves, our lives often go on, day after day, having little meaning or value. Eventually we realize that we cannot afford to spend our entire lives on a seesaw of pleasure and pain, and that true fulfillment comes by giving up our grasping and finding contentment within ourselves.

No matter how our lives may seem on the surface, problems always exist at deeper, more subtle levels of consciousness. There are various methods we can use to bring them to the surface; but as soon as we think we have solved one problem, more frustrations or dissatisfactions set in. It is like digging in sand on the beach—as soon as we remove a handful of water, more water seeps in. So, we just continue to get trapped in an endless progression of problems, temporary solutions, and more problems. We can relieve some of the surface tension by emotional outbursts—and once these are over, we may even feel a little lighter or more relaxed. But this is like shifting weight from one place to another; the problem still remains, even though we may wishfully sense a change for the better. Because the underlying causes have not been resolved, the same problems or patterns continue to occur.

We may decide to fight these negative forces, but fighting often just perpetuates the negative energies and further alienates us from ourselves. It seem that the more we fight our negativity, the stronger it becomes.

So we somehow need to find a positive approach to deal with our problems. But first we need to understand that consciousness is only a collection of habit patterns. No matter how fixed or persistent they may seem, the patterns are not solid or substantial—we can change and rearrange them. Negative reactions create forces which form a pattern; but this pattern can be broken. Once we understand the way habit patterns operate within the mind, and once the process of awakening awareness begins, then awareness penetrates and transforms our problems and obstacles. When we are mindful, instead of getting lost in conflict and indulging ourselves in misery, self-condemnation, or self-indulgent melancholy, we can quickly and easily see through our difficulties and transmute negative energy into positive energy. This takes some practice, but when we use intrinsic awareness to learn to see and quickly change destructive situations, our problems clear up, and peace and light begin to grow within us.

When problems arise in meditation or in daily life, when we are overly emotional or trapped in a pattern of behavior which causes us to suffer, that is the time to practice openness and balance, and to awaken mindfulness. For example, when we are extremely sad or angry, if we concentrate properly on the emotion, looking at it intensely from above and below, and then facing it directly, it can actually disappear—because we see that it is really 'nothing'. With practice, we can quickly balance a depressing or frustrating situation by switching the mind back and forth—making it happy, making it sad, making it happy again—all the time watching what is happening inside ourselves. First, we can do something positive, then something negative. One time, switch the mind to depression and really cry. Then, immediately switch to laughter. What, really, are these emotions? Why should I be controlled by these transitory mental states?

This exercise may seem almost schizophrenic, but as we work on it we discover that an important change takes place within our consciousness and in the way we look at ourselves and the world. Sadness is not so serious and happiness is not so frivolous.

*L*ife is moving and changing much faster than even a few years ago. Many exciting and fascinating things are happening every day—it is all a very beautiful dance, and every situation, every activity, and every thought has its place in our practice. Each experience can teach us how foolish it is to be so dramatic and serious—and that even our difficulties can be transcended, for nothing is permanent.

Yet at the same time, this realization is not easy to put into practice. We are so tied up in negative patterns that we may even be strengthening our negative emotions without knowing we are doing so. When we are unaware, when we are sad, depressed, or unhappy, we are like bees trapped in a jar—they buzz around in restless patterns, with no way of escape. Yet we are not completely trapped. Our emotional problems and negative attitudes are in one way part of our learning process.

By means of awareness we can become sensitive to our emotions as they arise and thus begin to break our emotional patterns and our attachments to them. The more our awareness increases, the more time we have for positive action; three weeks for the person who is aware are the same as three months for the person who is not. When we remind ourselves to keep our bodies and minds in harmony with our awareness, we become familiar with every change in our thoughts and moods; and we can remember to bring our awareness immediately into the midst of any situation that could disturb our balance. This practice is like learning to swim; once we learn the first strokes, with practice we will gradually be able to swim—not just for five or ten minutes, but for as long as we like. Similarly, we can develop continuous meditation if we sustain an open attitude in whatever activities we are involved.

Because anxiety causes, consciously or unconsciously, many of our problems, it is important to deal with it as soon as it arises. The best antidote to anxiety is meditation. When we learn to control the emotions through meditation, we become less burdened by our problems; our bodies and minds become very still, and anxiety starts to disolve in calm relaxation and quiet. We can then begin to work with our problems directly, for we no longer feel the need to escape them. Our tenseness and blockages naturally ease. Thus, we are no longer caught in a cycle of craving and anxiety, and we can enjoy living in our bodies and minds. This is the first stage of meditation.

Attaining Inner Confidence

Once we go through a true process of self-discovery,
no one can take away our self-confidence;
the inspiration comes from within,
and we know without needing to be told.

Spiritual confidence is more difficult to attain than worldly confidence. We can easily learn to drive a car, fix a lawnmower, or talk informatively on a variety of subjects. But how can we learn to attain inner confidence? There are no specific steps to follow. Yet, by utilizing the insight, strength, and confidence gained from meditation we naturally discover the truth which is always within us. And in becoming more confident of our experience, we come to see that devotional or sentimental beliefs are not so important. We learn to believe and trust in ourselves.

When we look at our ordinary experience with an attitude of openness, free from judgments or divisive concepts, we see 'subject' and 'object' naturally as one. In this way, the spiritual path becomes a part of our lives —not just an abstract ideal reserved for special occasions. When meditative experience is truly a part of us, spiritual qualities naturally express themselves in our daily lives, and we can be confident that our meditative awareness will carry us through whatever situations we encounter.

Once this inspiration and self-confidence becomes our teacher, and once we contact this inner guide, we can always rely on our experience and realization, rather than on what is outside ourselves. Our daily lives give us the substance of our learning process. *There* is the raw material—our flesh, our breath, our environment. When we learn to accept and appreciate ourselves without selfishness or ego-grasping, instead of floundering in negativity and self-condemnation, we begin to evolve positive qualities—strength, confidence, and feelings of inner lightness.

Yet, although the potential for enlightenment is always within us, most of us do not experience it. We are trapped by our dualistic minds. Cultures and religions tend to teach a dualistic view of existence, and most of us have difficulties freeing ourselves from the rigid concepts of these systems. Because of our basic tendency to polarize experience, we forget to use our awareness in difficult situations. We become 'attached' to a problem and let it control our minds, or we feel that we have to evaluate the situation. We waste time and energy. However, as our meditative experience deepens, we feel less need to discriminate and judge. We begin to transcend our dualistic tendencies by developing stability and balance, and by realizing that spiritual truth is found in ourselves and our daily lives.

We may have some idea that a place of ultimate understanding exists—but heaven is not necessarily somewhere else. It is within the nature of our minds, and this we reach through meditation. We just accept each situation as it comes, and follow our inner guidance—our intuition, our own hearts.

In order to awaken mindfulness and improve our awareness, it is useful to examine our self-image and personality by asking ourselves, "Where am I? What am I doing?" This can help us stay 'within' the meditation and can increase our attentiveness to the specific situations in which we find ourselves. It can bring us out of cloudy mental dialogues and image-building, and thus help us to live more full and meaningful lives.

To be sure our meditation or awareness has a firm foundation, we can check it from time to time. When we are meditating in a very quiet setting, our minds may seem very positive, calm, and peaceful—but when we go out into the world, to our homes or offices, or when we encounter difficult or threatening situations, we may find that negative emotions can still overpower us. But rather than avoiding these situations or trying to hide from them, we can learn to welcome them and use them—for they can help us to test and strengthen the insight and the power of our meditation.

It is even possible to have peak experiences during moments of anxiety, anger, or resentment, for the basic energy is there, ready to be transformed. As the potential for realization is inherent within our minds, it is also within the emotions themselves. This potential is in every instant of our lives, and through meditation we can learn to reach it.

One helpful practice is to meditate equally on our positive and negative feelings—not holding to that which feels good or avoiding that which is painful. In this way, we can discover and use the positive qualities that exist even within the negativities of our minds. We then no longer feel the need to identify with or reject any of our emotions; we experience them directly, not discriminating between them. By developing and improving our awareness, we can transcend our negative emotions; they begin to lose their hold on us, and we start to feel lighter and more confident. Through these experiences we can even penetrate the nature of reality . . . and at these rare moments, we can experience great joy.

C onstant awareness of whatever we are doing is even more important than formal meditation or practice, for when we are mindful every moment, our confidence and balance increase. And eventually we will understand how crucial every thought, word, and action is both for ourselves and for others.

As we extend this understanding into our daily lives, we can learn to sustain a quality of openness continually. When we remain open, alert, and mindful, our emotions and problems are not able to overpower us. We can allow them to arise without grasping at them and thus we no longer get caught in emotional thunderstorms.

Just as scientists test their theories in laboratories, we can test ourselves in daily life. When we are balanced and satisfied and find that our minds are clear and our hearts are open, then we know we are beginning to contact the truth within ourselves.

Sustaining our faith and trust is one of the most important parts of developing a spiritual life. Anyone can sustain an interest for a short period of time or even for a year or two, but the more complex and conflicting the world becomes, the more difficult it is to survive spiritually—to survive internally—because everything seems to lure us away from meditation and inner calm, from our sense of inner strength and wisdom. At times we may become discouraged with our meditation practice and think that we are just wasting our time and energy; that nothing is really happening and that we should just give it up. But it is important to be mindful of every action, in each situation, and encourage ourselves, for even one negative thought can reverse our direction. Each moment has the potential for enlightenment, but each moment also has the potential to be destructive.

When the world seems to be continually indulging itself in endless sensations and fascinations, we can protect ourselves and our integrity by firmly deciding to guide ourselves away from unwholesome or enmeshing influences. It is important to listen to our inner guidance rather than be swayed by others, for we can very easily drift away from even our strongest realizations and determinations for positive action. So, we need to sustain our initial dedication to the truth, no matter what may occur—emotional storms or threatening situations. The person who is committed to truth and genuine understanding never gives up; this tenacity is one of the most important foundations for discovering reality.

Sometimes even intelligent people get caught in the pattern of mindlessly following others. If this happens to us, over a period of time we can lose our original self-confidence and balance, and we may even begin to feel like a failure. Once this weakness manifests, we become vulnerable to negative emotions and destructive situations which pull us further off balance. It is like an infection which is very hard to cure. Our psychological conflicts become so entrenched that our minds spin endlessly in circles.

Once we reject our inner guidance, it is not easy to find it again, because our views and motivations may have changed. So, like a person groping in the dark who finds a sure guide, once we make contact with our strength and awareness, we should not let it go. This is important, because there are times when we feel weak or especially vulnerable. It is not always easy to have faith in our own judgment, but when we follow the truth as we understand it, we learn to be confident in ourselves and enjoy each moment. When we have lived our lives in this way, we will be able to look back and realize how much we have learned and accomplished, and how fortunate we are to have gained so much understanding. Even now, we know enough to have confidence in ourselves—and this is a tremendous source of guidance and protection.

Each day, we can expand our openness so that awareness flows freely and naturally. We do not need any other preparation. We may try to meditate for many years without success; but with this openness, in a very short time, we can learn to meditate perfectly with no trouble at all. When we meditate with such openness and leave all doubts and hesitations behind, our inner guidance automatically leads us to the teachings within. The more our awareness develops, the more we open to spontaneous mind experience.

One of my teachers once explained that great fighters, such as the samurai, perfect every move, every gesture before they engage in battle, so that when they encounter the enemy, they are completely prepared. They have no doubt about how to maneuver; they no longer even think about it. They just do it, and every move is automatically perfect.

Similarly, in meditation, until we have complete confidence and there are no questions left, everything is practice and preparation. No matter what we are doing, we can practice staying in awareness, in the spontaneous, present moment. There is no need to ask, how is it? What is it? Who is it? We learn just to meditate perfectly without any restrictions or second thoughts.

We might ask, then, why we need preliminary physical and mental purification and why we need to learn specific techniques. These practices are needed because it is so difficult to directly penetrate the 'secret path' of meditation. However, once we understand meditation, once we have the key, we can intuitively remain in that state of awareness no matter what we do.

When we have discovered for ourselves something of value, it will always stay with us; we will not get this certainty from anyone else. So we should develop confidence and encourage ourselves, realizing that our lives are very precious and that our ordinary experience is the true path of knowledge. When we know that what we are doing is 'right' and that we are attaining our goal, we stop depending upon others, and truly begin to appreciate our lives.

As we practice meditation and test our experience, we learn the meaning of the saying, "Truth is like gold: the more it is burned and beaten, the finer its quality becomes." Once we go through a true process of self-discovery, no one can take away our self-confidence; the inspiration comes from within, and we *know* without needing to be told. In some ways this is the only teaching that makes sense, and it is always there for us to consult, because truth is transmitted through self-knowledge. So, we can remind ourselves to remain confident—confident in our meditation and confident in our experience.

Discovering Mind

*We can experience the mind
as alive, sensitive, and brilliant . . .
like radiant sunlight.*

Until we are able to actually understand our minds, we remain strangers to ourselves, unconscious of our true potential. We may spend many years attempting to learn the nature of the mind, but in fact, whatever we experience *is* the mind. This does not mean that external objects are our minds, but rather that our projections of experience themselves are a part of the mind.

If I were to go back to Tibet and someone were to ask me, "What is American culture like, can you tell me?" I could not do so in just a few words. Similarly, there are many different ways to explain mind, for mind is experienced differently by various individuals, and there are countless types, degrees, and levels of mind to consider.

The mind is very versatile, like an artist—creating confusion, delusion, and suffering, as well as great order and surpassing beauty. It projects all form and supports all our inner dramas; it can manifest absolute truth as well as all our thoughts and emotions. Mind is not one thing, or many things, or anything in itself. We may use various words to describe the scope of the mind and to discuss its apparent functioning; sometimes we may label mind 'consciousness' and sometimes 'awareness', but the more we investigate and observe, the more complex the mind appears to be.

Most interpretations of the mind are limited because they relate mind to some other concept—mind is like this, consciousness is like that. In dealing with the mind, our egos categorize our experience of the world into specific forms, structures, and outlines. These become strict patterns which govern our existence, like the constitution governs the country. They are, however, superimposed upon the mind; they are not the mind itself.

Often, in trying to discover the nature of the mind, we make the mistake of chasing after meanings. We feel that if we understand the *meaning* of certain concepts, words, or experiences, then we have gained a foothold on real knowledge. But meanings depend upon other concepts, and have no substantial foundation themselves. Searching for meaning can thus become a self-perpetuating cycle; we become like a cat chasing its tail, or like a runner who hyperventilates and can no longer control his breath.

Because there is little specific data on the inner workings of the mind, it is difficult to discover much accurate knowledge about the mind. We may look at mind in its physical sense as related only to the brain and to a series of neurological patterns. Or, intellectually, we may be interested in how perception functions through the physical senses or how we formulate concepts or make decisions. As we investigate mind from a meditative point of view, we see that mind is much more than the brain or a filter for perceptions, much more than just

a collection of concepts. Through meditation we can go beyond meanings and categories into direct experience of the inner levels of mind. We can experience the mind as alive, sensitive, and brilliant . . . like radiant sunlight.

Consciousness, or simple awareness, deals with sensations, perceptions, images, and emotions, but these are just fragments which, added together, do not make up the whole mind. Mind is far vaster than all these things put together. Buddhist psychology posits over fifty specific mental events and at least eight different states of consciousness, yet even these are just the surface level of mind. We can go beyond consciousness to discover the non-conceptual levels of mind; we can examine *all* the layers, like removing the petals of a rose. We can examine the mind beyond the substance level—even beyond the existence or non-existence level—because mind is unimaginably vast.

As we investigate the mind more deeply, we discover that mind itself has no substance. It has no color and no shape, no form, no position, no characteristics, no beginning, and no end. It is neither within nor without, and thus it cannot be pinpointed as this or that. It is not mixed together with other things, yet it is not separate from them. The mind cannot be invented, destroyed, rejected, or accepted. It is beyond reasoning and logical processes, beyond ordinary time and all existence.

As we practice meditation we begin to recognize the tremendous activity which goes on in the mind. We can begin to work with particular thoughts and problems, and as we go through the process of confronting, accepting, suppressing, or changing these, we can gain an understanding about the mind and the way it works.

One of the major obstacles to discovering and appreciating the depth and quality of the mind is that we take our minds for granted and do not properly respect them. This respect need not be in an egotistical manner, but it is very important to realize how valuable and precious our minds are. Usually, whenever positive experiences occur to us, we praise the ego rather than the mind, for we consider the ego as the agent of the intellect. Yet, when problems or difficulties occur we blame the mind; we give names to our various neuroses, and accept them as real and as part of the mind, although the mind itself is innocent. This rejection of the mind as something foreign and even harmful to us is not a healthy attitude. We often show great concern for our bodies, beautifying ourselves and creating impressive self-images, yet seldom do we equally appreciate the spectrum, realm, and totality of our minds.

The mind is the source of all knowledge and inspiration. When we become enlightened it is the mind that is enlightened; when we are sad it is mind that is sad. As we begin to appreciate and respect our minds, we find that mind itself can transform our daily experience. Our problems appear as less real—for we discover that all our problems are actually self-created. The more we investigate our minds, the more we go beyond problems, beyond words and concepts . . . to discover truth and understanding. We need not blindly follow anyone else's ideas, but can explore our own minds to greater and greater depth until we discover the nature of the mind—which is illuminating, radiant, alive.

The Natural State of Mind

*Since mind in its true nature
is without duality, not separate
from the unity of all that is,
our lives become our meditation.*

Those who are not accustomed to meditation often feel it is something foreign, unusual, or unnatural —an exotic experience to be achieved—or that meditation is somehow different from the person meditating, or that it is just another facet of Eastern psychology or philosophy to be researched, studied, and explored. Meditation, however, is not something foreign, separate, or external. Meditation is the natural state of mind, and the whole nature of the mind can be our meditation.

Meditation begins when we allow our bodies and minds to relax deeply and fully . . . which we do by experiencing the feeling that comes from simply letting go, without even having told ourselves to do so. When we let everything be just as it is and listen to the silence within our minds—this becomes our meditation. This silence is not just absence of sound or even freedom from distraction; it is full openness, the presence of the mind. When we simply remain silent within the moment—

without grasping for security, without trying to figure out our problems—all that remains is awareness.

Meditation is the process of self-discovery. On one level the meditation experience shows us the patterns of our lives—how we have carried on our emotional characteristics since childhood. But on another level it frees us from these patterns, making it easier for us to see our inner potentials. When we look *backward* at the patterns of our thoughts, we can sometimes observe and identify the deceptions created by our self-images. We can learn to see through the mind's posturings and pretenses and through all our explanations and excuses. We can realize we are still just playing games and are far from genuine self-knowledge.

We continually set arbitrary limits and restrictions on ourselves by looking at and experiencing the world from rigid viewpoints; we think an experience that is not related to our senses or projections has no value. But when we go beyond objectifying concepts, beyond dualism, beyond space and time, what is there to lose? If anything, just our fears, our fixed ideas, our tense clinging to an imagined 'I' and that I's imagined security. The natural state of mind has nothing to lose. It is only because of our alienation from ourselves that we have previously failed to realize that we can abide within awareness, which is our intrinsic nature, our own home.

Although we 'talk' about our intrinsic self-nature, this does not necessarily mean that we experience it. Instead, most of us are continually caught up in the process of generating ideas and explanations which create more ideas and explanations . . . our minds going on almost endlessly. The 'I' is always associating itself with various feelings, concepts, and psychological reflections. The ego is always waiting to ask us if we have achieved anything; so we have to 'report back' to ourselves all the time—and we find ourselves outside our experience looking in.

Although we try our best to be mindful and aware, our inner dialogues and projections create obstacles which spoil the immediacy of our experience. The more we try to interpret an experience and clothe it in words, the more we remove ourselves from it. We are left with 'fixed' concepts, and dualistic views concerning the world, so that our responses and reactions to daily situations do not flow from a natural state. It is as if we were to live in the middle of a beautiful flower garden —and yet be unaware of it. Years and years can be spent, explaining, thinking, and analyzing, but never discovering this natural state.

Realizing this state of mind is difficult, because we believe that our thoughts and feelings are 'mine'; we judge them in relation to 'my' situation, 'my' life. But thoughts and feelings are not 'me' at all. One thought simply is associated with another thought, and then another. We go a little deeper and find still another. Each thought involves various words and images, like motion picture frames which are moving continuously, forward or backward, so that the imagery occupies our awareness and drains our energy. Finally, awareness is lost. We become like children watching cartoons—just lost there, staring.

As we observe our minds, we see that our consciousness easily becomes fixed on thoughts or sensory input. For example, when we suddenly hear a door slam or traffic screech, our minds immediately project an image or concept; and associated with this idea or image is an experience with very precise and exact feeling tones. By staying within the immediate moment, it is possible to

enter 'within' this experience. At that moment we discover a certain type of inner atmosphere or environment
that has no shape, no form, no specific characteristic or
structure. There are no words, images, concepts, or
positions to hold, because any position at all—a holding
position, an examining position, or even a 'beyond' position would still be referring to something that is ultimately related to ourselves as the subject. Therefore to
become free from the dualistic patterns of our minds, it is
important to go 'beyond' relative understandings and
beliefs, to look *inside*, and, as much as possible, to stay
within the very first moment of experience.

S ince mind in its true nature is without duality,
not separate from the unity of all things, our
lives become our meditation. Meditation is not a technique for escaping this world—it is a good friend and
teacher who can guide, support, and help our minds to
touch our innermost beings directly, with no walls to
divide us from our awareness, inspiration, and intuition. Through this experience we can contact our own
wholeness.

So every moment, we can make friends with
meditation; and in the view arising from meditation, we
can experience all existence as full and beautiful—for
everything has beauty, the way we work, think, talk—
every situation has its own inherent value and meaning.
When we bring the light of meditation into our lives,
they become richer, more meaningful and purposeful,
and we are able to deal with all situations openly and
directly.

This natural awareness is simple and direct, open and
responsive. It is immediate and spontaneous, without

obscuration; there is no fear or guilt, no problem or desire to escape or be any other way. 'Natural' means 'unfixed', to have no expectations, no compulsions, no interpretations, or predetermined plans. When meditation deepens, there is no need to fix it, improve it, or perfect it. There is no need to progress, since everything moves on in the natural state of reality.

Once we are able to experience this immediate awareness, there is nothing between our minds and meditation. The experience is always new, fresh, clear, and beautiful. Though it is beyond our ordinary sense of time, still there is continuity. Everything is just 'as it is', with nothing added or subtracted.

If, in our meditation, we can stay in the present moment, it is possible to experience this higher state of awareness. But when we hold on to mental projections or try to remember specific instructions or certain processes, we only continue to follow the movements of the mind at the consciousness level. We may study and practice on a conceptual level for years, perform many positive actions, and collect a great deal of information, but still not come much closer to real understanding. Therefore, it is necessary to expand awareness out of the realm of inner dialogue, to loosen and open up as much as we can, and to become very silent. These are still just concepts, but later on, with practice, we can go beyond these ideas and conceptual patterns to a state which is completely centerless, because all limitations that necessitate a center have dissolved—and this is meditation.

As we develop meditation, we no longer need to rely on intellectual explanations to justify who we are, for our restricting self-identity fades away, like fog touched by sunlight. Once we understand this, we do not need to struggle with our egos and negative emotions—or with discriminations of good or bad, positive or negative, spiritual path or habitual action. Within the meditation experience, spontaneous awareness arises by itself, and emotional conflicts and problems begin to lose their holding power and become very cloud-like. Once we stop feeding our problems, they disappear within awareness itself. At that time we can truly see that the whole nature of the mind is our meditation. And through this our minds become illumined with a powerful, precious energy, and we directly experience an indescribable, all-knowing understanding.

Becoming the
Meditation Experience

*When we meditate properly
we can do it with great concentration,
and yet, at the same time,
not make any effort.*

If you have any questions—on anything at all—I would
like to hear them. Someone said to me, "Well, meditation seems simple . . ." but if you have any questions
about your meditation, your experience or daily life, and
if I can help in clarifying anything, I am here. We have
this time in which to talk and share with each other.

Student: When I meditate, should I continue using the
mantra I learned from another teacher?
Rinpoche: That's up to you. If a mantra helps you to
contact a deeper level of meditation, you may want to
continue to use it. Mantras can help us to relax, and there
are also devotional aspects to mantra which can aid in
developing our inner qualities.

   Mantras can be very powerful 'tools' for helping the
mind concentrate and avoid being distracted. On the
other hand, since the mind is still engaged in an 'exercise', saying mantras may limit us by holding our atten-

tion to subject and object discriminations. So each of us must decide for ourselves when a mantra is helpful and when it is not.

Mantras are also used in the visualization of certain colors and forms. When we practice mantras either aloud or silently for long continuous periods, even after we stop chanting they can continue to vibrate within us on more subtle levels. Mantras have very powerful effects and are useful in healing both physical and mental difficulties.

Student: Is there a special meditation for healing?

Rinpoche: Meditation *is* self-healing. It is a process of more fully understanding our minds and our own natures. Through analyzing the mind we can learn how we process information and how we respond to specific situations. When the mind is still, like a pond, we can calmly watch the ripples come and go. We can also see the reflection of all our self-images, and eventually, when the 'watcher', as well as our thoughts, disappear, we can experience the mind directly.

In meditation we first try to 'pin down' mind, to hold it so that we can observe it. But as our meditation develops, we can begin to relax, let go, and just *be*— without effort and without grasping. At that time we discover that the 'mind' itself does not exist; it is nowhere to be found. This natural state of direct experience is our self-healer.

Student: I read an article about a doctor who was using meditation and visualization to cure cancer patients.

Rinpoche: This is not surprising. Certain illnesses are the result of blockages in our physical bodies caused by our emotions. Once we become very relaxed through meditation it is possible to transform the illness. In Tibet there were very few cases of cancer because the environment was quiet and peaceful—life was much easier and so there was less disease. Even so, everyone must eventually face illness and death.

Here the environment is often crowded and noisy, and it is difficult to find a peaceful place, so the only solution seems to be to find our own inner peace. Modern technology has given us many conveniences, but our needs and habits trap us and become so much a part of our lives that we cannot give them up. Though technology has brought some comfort, it has not cured our frustrations. We encounter so much material wealth and have so many alternatives that many of us are very confused by it all. Even if we struggle very hard for a whole lifetime, putting great energy into our work, we may produce only very limited results. We seem to be caught in a cycle of pleasure and pain, expectation and disappointment. So why does this have to happen?

There is a story about two brothers. One was mean, but very smart; the other was very stubborn and also very stupid. One day they were both running in a field. The mean brother decided to have some fun and said, "You sit here in the valley and I will go into the hills and send you back a big present. It will make strange crackling and whitching noises, but you have to hold it until I get back." So he climbed up a hill, found a large white rock, heated it until it was red hot, and then rolled it down the hill, yelling, "Hey, Brother, here's your present. Catch it! Don't let go until I come back!"

The stupid brother was so anxious to get a present that he ran and caught the rock. The fur on the animal skin he was wearing crackled and whitched as it burned. The rock burned through the animal skin and then burned him all over, but he still did not drop it. He thought the rock valuable. So he talked to the rock, saying, "Whatever you do to me, I won't give you up until my brother comes." And he stubbornly held on to it because he thought it was important to him.

We hold on to all that we love in the same way, even though it can be extremely frustrating and painful. We also hold on to our meditation, wanting to see colors and visions, have warm feelings and sensations, and experience the higher stages. Our minds still want to identify, capture, and manipulate experience so as to have something enjoyable to report back to ourselves. Yet once we let go of our attachment to senses and feelings, we can *become* the experience itself—and this is the real healing process.

Student: Do you consider anger bad?
Rinpoche: Anger is not necessarily either good or bad . . . it depends upon your interpretation. But anger does destroy your peace and balance. Its energy is sharp and it increases emotional reactions, so a deeper, more natural harmony is lost, and the result is upsetting and dissatisfying. But on a higher level, whoever knows how to use the energy from meditation can use anger as a source of energy to develop a deeper, clearer meditation.

Student: When I get really angry and give it some sort of expression—if it is not too explosive—I feel a kind of peace afterward.
Rinpoche: That is not completely true. The person who releases anger has been holding and repressing it for some time. When he lets it go, he feels physical relief at the stimulation of certain blocked body energies, and this feels temporarily exhilarating. But the deeper anger, the

source of the anger, does not dissolve, and in some ways it becomes stronger because it has found a way to demand control and express itself. So it will come back again. The peace is only temporary, an illusion—the cause of the deeper dissatisfaction still needs to be resolved.

Student: Can't anger be seen as a healthy expression, as a working out of a natural process?

Rinpoche: Yes, in a way, emotions are natural; but what does 'natural' really mean? We all behave according to various patterns—our body, speech, and mind each have particular patterns. We categorize these as good or bad, right or wrong, according to how well they work for us. Our culture and society also follow certain patterns which may or may not agree with what we want or think best.

Every human being has accumulated physical and psychological blockages or patterns which are very difficult to break. When we try to free ourselves of these personal or cultural patterns of behavior, we may be considered abnormal or even crazy. Yet, even behavior considered 'natural' or 'normal' according to our cultural or private situations is not necessarily positive or healthy.

Student: Could you say something about sexual feelings?

Rinpoche: We can enjoy sex, feel relaxed and satisfied, or we may end up with great dissatisfaction. Very much depends on each individual and the total relationship. Sex can be very healing when there is no ego involved. If one is very sensitive and can totally relax—not bound by possessiveness, craving, or selfish attachment—then sexuality can be very liberating.

Most of the time, however, sexual feeling involves a craving—it needs something tangible to touch, and as soon as the craving is fulfilled it just disappears.

Sex by itself does not seem to have that much value. In a way, human beings are unfortunate—we have very few pleasures, and they do not last long. There are so many interruptions and difficulties, so many problems, and we often end up frustrated or only partially fulfilled. It seldom seems quite right. There is a superficial fascination but not what we would call 'happiness'.

Trying to relieve our tensions and feelings is like trying to scratch a rash underneath our skin—though it seems to relieve the itch, the irritation is still there, underneath. That is why we say that the nature of our ordinary human situation is dissatisfaction. Somehow we have to learn to find satisfaction in each present moment, rather than in brief or sensational encounters.

Student: I somehow never feel really satisfied with myself.
Rinpoche: You are not the only one. Most of us are that way.

Student: Is that something everyone just lives with then, or is there a way to find some peace?
Rinpoche: There are times when we are happy for short periods, just as there are times when we are rather passive, not particularly aware of anything. But we cannot sustain our happy feelings, and often do not even know where they have gone. Our futures, too, become repetitions of our pasts. Even though we are not very happy, we continue to behave in the same way, hoping that the future will somehow be different, and finally—life is over. Some of us are not happy, but we do not even

realize it. At least you are aware that you are sometimes not satisfied. That is actually the beginning of the way out.

Student: Are emotions and feelings the same?

Rinpoche: Emotions and feelings are basically different. When we first contact an object through our senses, we may have an initial or intuitive 'feeling' about it, but immediately we judge it, categorize it, and cover up what it *is* with how we want it to be. This is part of our human pattern of conceptualization. Eventually, we want to go beyond this level of interpretation and become more sensitive to the experience itself.

Emotions have more force than feelings and are more volitional, whereas feelings do not have that much force and are more physical. But we need to experience these distinctions rather than just analyze them; it is not enough simply to watch our emotions and physical sensations. Our experience itself is what is important.

In the West, it seems that when people talk about the 'mind' what they are referring to is not 'mind' or 'consciousness', but only the mind as a channel for the senses. In other words, according to the Western way of thinking, 'mind-experience' or 'consciousness-experience' is still just another subtle form of feeling. However, the 'mind' is beyond sensation.

Student: Sometimes I find that after meditating I feel good, and at other times I feel tired.

Rinpoche: It is possible that you are trying too hard, making too much effort. Perhaps you are a little too intense— great seriousness can make one a little tired. When you tighten your muscles, tense your body, or direct your energy in certain forced ways, that, too, can make you a little tired, so just take a few deep breaths, relax, and loosen up. Let go of the thoughts that are running around in your head and creating tension or worry.

There are times when you are naturally calm and relaxed, when you enjoy meditation and are at peace. At other times you may be sleepy, or mentally experience either very dark or very light places. No matter what happens you need to be alert *all* of the time, but careful not to fasten your mind rigidly on anything. Meditation is a delicate process, which is why it is essential to learn how to meditate properly from the very beginning; otherwise, it can take a long time to fully contact awareness. And the best way to begin is to relax.

Student: Is it a good idea to stop meditating when you are tired?

Rinpoche: Well, you have several options. When you are tired or sleepy and your mind is wandering, it may help to do physical exercises for awhile—walking, breathing, or stretching to increase your circulation and to loosen muscle tension—and then sit again. Also, you can loosen up mentally, get rid of whatever tensions or problems you might have, try to penetrate any blockages and go beyond them.

Student: Should one set a time as to how long to meditate?

Rinpoche: It depends on the individual. Some people prefer a disciplined structure and like to meditate for a set time every day, in a specific place, and in a certain position. Others would rather meditate a little bit whenever they have time. But it is most important to learn to be mindful at all times; then meditative awareness inspires everything you do.

Student: Is the position important?

Rinpoche: The cross-legged posture is traditional but not necessary—there were no chairs in India, and people sat cross-legged from early childhood on.

In one way, however, position is very important. Physiologically, an erect posture is very valuable because it provides stillness of body and makes possible a flow of certain energies. But once again posture depends upon your preference. A certain position may be very uncomfortable, and if your mind is always wandering to that pain, it may be better to change positions or to massage yourself and do certain exercises in order to relax and meditate comfortably. On the other hand, sometimes you need to go into the pain, concentrate on it, and learn to go beyond it.

Student: Does perseverance require going against something that is not natural?

Rinpoche: We may have to persevere against various obstacles if our natural state is out of balance or disturbed. On the other hand, a person with higher understanding can always find natural states within perseverance itself.

Our effort is always influenced by our 'self', and when there is no longer any perseverance, there is no longer any self. First we understand this, then we experience it; or we may have the experience first, leading to the understanding. But if we have experience without understanding, it is quickly forgotten, like a sudden flash of lightning. Therefore, we need guidance.

Student: Do you see the need to try to protect yourself before you meditate, so that you do not pick up negative energy?

Rinpoche: It is possible for you to pick up negative energy when you 'walk' into the 'meditation fields', but the person who is confident can transmute the negative vibrations into a good experience, like recyling.

Student: When you receive energy from meditation practice, how do you release it?

Rinpoche: This is a natural process, and so there is no need to worry or be concerned about it. Just be open and do not try to concentrate forcefully. The way to release the energy is not to evaluate the experience, not to identify it with your 'self', and not to take so seriously whatever is happening at the moment.

Learn to feel that all existence is part of a dream. You are both the dreamer and the dream being dreamed. Feel, relax, let yourself be loose, and do not meditate too intensely. During meditation 'nobody' is meditating, nobody is there to comment or wait for information. Information indicates judgment—good or bad meditation, happy or unhappy feelings—all of which are reflections of some 'one' watching from the background. A rocket being launched needs to report back information on its success or failure, but in meditation there is no need for feedback. Feedback merely disturbs meditation. When you are free from hopes or expectations, then meditation is flowing, neither rigid nor serious. Yet, in a sense, you *are* serious, because you are practicing very concentratedly and very alertly.

Student: Meditation seems to require effort, and yet you emphasize complete relaxation.

Rinpoche: When we meditate properly we can do it with great concentration, and yet, at the same time, not make any effort. In other words, we do not 'fix' our minds on anything, since there is nothing to focus upon, nothing to aim towards, no need to make any effort. Still, if we do not start and continue, there is no progress. We *do* have to do something, but the doing is almost not-doing, because there is nothing for the 'self' to do—there is no self to do anything.

Nowadays, there is an emphasis on figuring out how to do everything, and this makes it difficult to understand what 'natural' is, what 'meditation' is, what the 'absolute' is. Although there is nothing to be figured out, still we need to develop a very sharp, clear, and accurate awareness. Then once the 'I' steps away, we can experience 'meditation'. But then again, we may delude ourselves by thinking that our meditation is going well, while in fact this thinking itself is a subtle grasping at a 'position' in our meditation and is thus actually keeping us from meditating.

Once we relax, we should let the mind be completely open, with a balanced, free energy. The mind is always so animated. We become attached to certain ways of thinking, looking, and expressing ourselves—both to please ourselves and others. These are all part of the self-image perpetuating itself; once we step away from the self-image, our minds will be free to 'meditate'.

Student: Do you see a relationship between the results of meditation and creativity?

Rinpoche: Yes, I think so. When your mind is happy and at peace, then everything—all action—is creativity. Once your mind is in the meditative state of pure awareness—without restrictive judgments, concepts, or interpretations—then everything is art, is music, is beauty. Once you are liberated from negative views and fixed behavior patterns, all of your actions become open, spontaneous, and free. Every action of body and mind becomes a manifestation and expression of universal energy, which is intrinsically beautiful and joyful.

Few accomplished yogis, for example, do very much writing, drawing, singing, or playing music, because they are able to find beauty in all existence. Music is there, as well as art. All existence is an embodiment of truth; everything is naturally and intrinsically perfect, so there is no need for imitation or self-conscious effort.

When you perceive the universe from a particular perspective, your view is limited. But when you realize that it is all a universal energy field, you know that mind is infinite, and all existence is a part of 'heaven'. What 'heaven' actually means is that you have reached full understanding and you no longer cut yourself off from your experience. From this view, subject and object, positive and negative, the mundane and the supramundane all become one in equanimity.

Student: How can we know if we are growing spiritually?
Rinpoche: Spiritual growth is openness and fulfillment. Mostly we look for worldly freedom and satisfaction, but if there is no 'I', then who is being satisfied, who is being liberated? The total 'I' is liberated. Without 'I', without conflicting emotions, attitudes, and habits, we are free from all that binds us, but we may not report it to ourselves—the 'I' may not be there to listen. With 'I' it is very hard to develop; without 'I' we can progress. But without 'I', who is progressing? When people ask that of themselves, they sometimes become afraid.

Without the 'I' there is no subject, no object, no time. Some people may feel this is insane, but without the 'I' there is no one to go crazy, no demonic influence or person to react to it—only silent awareness. To arrive at this state we simply need to be open; we need make no extra effort. The right experiences are already happening when we do not allow ourselves to be distracted from our natural state of being. When we can remain balanced in the natural state of awareness, then nothing can harm us. We can function well and harmoniously without the 'support' of the ego.

Student: How can I free my meditation from the influence of the ego?

Rinpoche: The simple approach to meditation is that 'everything becomes meditation'. Do not think, "This is part of meditation; that is not part of meditation." There is no such differentiation. Meditate in the simplest, easiest, and most direct way. Be natural—naturally aware, naturally open, naturally alive. The more you try to figure it out intellectually, the longer it will take for you to understand. As long as you are self-conscious, it is not even good for you to meditate, because only the 'self' is meditating; and it is this 'self' who thinks it is meditating that keeps one from the actual meditation.

Once you understand natural awareness, every part of your mind is already within awareness. So the ego does not contaminate it, the ego does not pressure you, order you, or interrupt you.

Still, the ego is very clever. It is constantly seeking attention and relating each experience back to itself. This self-consciousness, or 'ego-thinking', always clings to an identity: 'my meditation, my awareness, my experience', dividing everything into subject and object.

There are various faces of ego—proud, dominating, threatening. Sometimes ego interprets experiences or defends itself; while at other times it formulates 'secret' intentions and maneuvers and then comments on them.

The ego has many aspects, creating channels through the senses—through the eyes, ears, and feelings.

When you enter the meditative state you do not need to rely on the senses; in fact you have the opportunity to transcend them. At the same time you can open the door of each sense—sight, sound, smell, taste, feeling, consciousness—all function harmoniously within the meditative state.

Student: How can you break down the ego?

Rinpoche: Dealing with the ego is like trying to touch the tail of a tiger—it is dangerous unless you know what you are doing. Often we are just playing when we attempt to confront our egos, so eventually we get hurt and come to resent ourselves deeply. In order to challenge the ego we must have skillful wisdom, being gentle at first and not directly fighting it, because when we fight it, we create frustrations which lead to more suffering. Instead, we need to *observe* the ego skillfully and directly, and as we observe it, we will see that fighting is not necessary.

We often blame everything on the ego, but as soon as we blame the ego we create conflict. There is conflict if we do not skillfully observe the ego, and conflict if we directly try to fight it. We may succeed in controlling the ego temporarily, but we may not be able to actually transcend it. If we cannot, then the ego will come back stronger and more full of resentment than it was before. Fighting and frustration become a polarity, perpetuating each other. We must touch the ego skillfully, rather than fight it. We need very sharp and clear self-observation.

Student: How are thoughts used?

Rinpoche: We deal with thoughts in two ways. When we 'grasp' thoughts, we identify but do not recognize them.

When we learn how to recognize thoughts, we begin to develop awareness.

Some people's thoughts are like snakes—they coil themselves into knots, but even these thoughts can be loosened. Snakes coil, but when they choose they can be completely loose, automatically relaxed.

When the mind is still, thoughts are like drawings on water—before we finish drawing, they flow away. Some people can see a thought when it arises, and then, like snow in California, it's gone before it touches the ground.

When we meditate our mind should be like Milarepa's cave—uncluttered. When Milarepa was living in a cave his single possession was a clay bowl in which he cooked nettles. Two hunters who had seen the smoke from his fire came to the cave at night to steal some food. When they began to search the cave, Milarepa laughed and said, "I am a yogi, and during the day I can find little to eat. How do you expect to find anything at night? This is a dark, empty place—there is nothing to take away." In the same manner, when we do not let our minds fill with thoughts, negative forces will have nothing to grasp, and so they cannot be of harm to us.

Student: Could you say something about mystical or esoteric experiences?
Rinpoche: There are often negative connotations associated with so-called 'mystical experience', and with anything which is private, secret, or 'occult'. But this 'secrecy' is misunderstood. If a certain growth or developing process is not yet complete, it is premature to talk about it or to concretize it. Therefore, in the long-range view, it is better to remain silent. Once our experience is completely established, we will never lose it; but until then it is important to keep silent. We need to cultivate what we have learned and allow it to grow and mature.

In order to understand these teachings, we have to experience them for ourselves and test them in our daily lives; this great potential—this inexhaustible treasury —is not in some distant land; it is within ourselves. That is why we speak about self-liberation and taking refuge in ourselves. The teachings themselves come alive within us. Once we know this, immediate experience becomes our teacher and awareness helps to make our lives positive and joyful.

When we look at life from the viewpoint of awareness, we see that our minds are a great source of protection; they can give us security and confidence; they can be our refuge. We can lose contact with awareness, and then gradually forget—yet awareness is accessible in every instant—we have one chance, then another chance —if we miss one, there is the next one. The mind is our home. But knowing that the mind is our home is not enough; we have to go through the door. Until we do, 'being' is just another word, like 'knowledge', 'wisdom', or 'esoteric'. Without experience, these words do not have much meaning.

Deeper meditation cannot be adequately expressed by language, for as soon as we verbalize or conceptualize experiences, they become solidified, and awareness stops. So until our practice is fully developed, it is better if we talk about our meditation experiences only with an accomplished guide who can help us; otherwise our experiences may lose their meaning and power.

Usually, however, we have a strong tendency to verbalize our experiences. We feel that unless we can interpret or discuss them, they are not real. We find it difficult to just let ourselves be silent, for silence disturbs us. Although talking about our problems and experiences can occasionally be useful, instead of helping us to integrate or understand them, talking can actually reinforce our attachments to them. Therefore, rather than following the impulse to verbalize our experiences either to ourselves or to others, it is usually best to silently work with them.

As soon as we use language and words to create concepts, we automatically dull and concretize the present; we then have no chance to experience that moment directly. There is no way we can go 'beyond' anything with words. This does not mean that words have no value, but only that there is no way we can experience the present moment directly if we rely on words, intellectual concepts, or attempts to focus our attention in certain ways.

So, from now on remember—every single thought is precious . . . the meaning is already present in the very first state. If you want to contact real mystical experience, it is not far from you; it is within your thoughts, within your awareness—within the very first moment. Explore this. As soon as you do, your whole attitude changes; your constricting, limiting, self-identity begins to fade, and your perceptions and images become transformed —it is like opening a window for fresh air.

Part Four

AWARENESS

Visualization and Seeing

*Visualization adds a new dimension
to our perception of the world and
gives us a new perspective with
which to view our ordinary reality.*

Visualization is very helpful in the development of awareness, concentration, and clarity. By focusing our consciousness on specific images or symbols, we can loosen the mental constructs that define and limit our perceptions. We thus become open to wider dimensions of experience and are less vulnerable to our emotions.

In more advanced meditation, when we are no longer so bound by subjects and objects, visualization can take place without form or structure. But as it takes a while before we learn to free our minds from dependence on dualistic thinking, when we are just beginning to develop concentration and visualization, it is useful to focus on specific objects.

Traditionally, both concentration and visualization start with focusing on a symbolic letter; they then move on to various symbols, images, mandalas, and deities, each with specific ornaments and qualities. We begin the process by concentrating on whatever we are visualizing for periods of ten or twenty minutes each day, until we reach a total of forty or fifty hours. As we look at the image very loosely, with our eyes completely relaxed and our breath and body very still, very receptive, the image eventually merges with our awareness.

Sometimes when we are just beginning our visualization practice, we may visualize well—but after a while the image may become unsteady or disappear altogether. More often, however, visualization is difficult at first, but as we continue, the image becomes more clearly focused and the visualization improves. Even then, we may find that when we try to visualize a specific image, a different image appears; and this can be disturbing. So we need to practice patiently, for it takes time to perfect these abilities.

A visualization first appears in front of us as though we were looking through a long tunnel or expandable tube. Although this seeing or awareness is very flexible, often we forget the image or become unconscious of it, so we are not able to perform the visualization accurately. Sometimes, however, when we close our eyes, what we are visualizing is just perfectly 'there'. Such a visualization does not need to be constructed piece by piece in the way that a carpenter builds a house; it arises spontaneously—a perfect image. Once we see it, we do not need to change anything. We can just let it be. And this spontaneity is the seed of visualization.

For example, try to inwardly visualize the healing color of turquoise blue—if you cannot see it, *feel* that you see it. This seeing is beautiful, so just accept it; and this acceptance will help you see it. If you still do not see it, then gently convince yourself that you are seeing perfectly, beautifully, and though you still may not see anything, feel the quality and the magnitude of the experience. Stay within the moment and the visualization will eventually come to you.

Visualization and imagination have some similarities. Imagination, however, is like memory or a mental projection, while visualization becomes spontaneous and is like seeing three dimensionally in all directions. Visualization is a finer, more highly developed, dynamic process. In imagination we can never quite contact the original brilliance of colors, shapes, sounds, and tastes —but visualizations are sometimes so sharp and radiant that they transcend our ordinary perceptions. In this field of visualization no object is mundane.

As we begin our visualization practice, the image is generally just a pale outline; gradually we can learn to focus the color and form more sharply. It is difficult to sharpen the complete visualization all at once, but gradually the colors become very vivid and clear—the light spectrum appears as rich and electrical color—and figures emerge not as lifeless images but as living forms.

As our abilities improve, our visualizations can be very complex—with many images becoming one, or one image becoming many. We can develop one single image or mandala to include the entire universe—everything fitting perfectly together. And we can begin to understand the nature of all existence and all phenomena— time, space, and knowledge. During visualization we may have extraordinary experiences which the rational mind cannot explain, but we know that what we are seeing is true, because we are experiencing the harmonious working of natural laws.

In visualization, first we look at form and color, but

later on the image enters our minds naturally, spontaneously. At first, we just watch the image as part of our meditation or concentration, but with practice, we can eventually train our minds so that we can see the image within ourselves. Later, we will not even need to look at a picture or close our eyes, and still we will see the image. It comes alive within our awareness.

In practicing visualization, we see with our awareness, not our eyes, and thus what we 'see' appears differently than in our ordinary sight. Although we begin by seeing an image or picture in a specific way, as we develop our visualization, the exact form of the image does not even matter, because the quality of 'seeingness' continues. The image itself is transcended, yet awareness remains and nourishes our minds and feelings; this awareness brings more meaning to our daily lives.

The purpose of visualization is to develop our awareness so that wherever we go or whatever we do, we become very mindful, and alert, like a deer's ear. Once we are familiar with the visualization process, we can compare our experience with our ordinary process of perception, and in this way gather information on how better to understand ordinary waking reality. We can arouse our awareness to see how delusion operates within the mind; we can develop this awareness to perceive all knowledge within our consciousness. So visualization adds a new dimension to our perception of the world and gives us a new perspective with which to view our ordinary reality.

The more we become accustomed to visualization practice, the more we become aware that what we call 'real' is itself like a visualization. This realization can change our whole way of thinking and increase our ability to see the transparent quality of the ego and of material objects. Once we see this, we can transform even our emotional obstacles into positive energy.

We can use this visualization 'seeingness' to concentrate on different levels of awareness in different centers of the body. This helps to open up the energies of our physical bodies and to release the tensions built up by the emotions. Often, in working with our problems, we view them from only one perspective or dimension, unable to see other alternatives. As a complex visualization may consist of only a single thought, we can begin to see how each thought can have many different qualities.

Through visualization, awareness can reveal three, four, and five dimensions to each experience—on one level, we might be experiencing physical pain; on another level, we may feel the pain as a kind of pleasurable sensation; on another level, the sensation may be felt as neutral, neither pain nor pleasure. On yet another level, nothing may be happening, for pain, pleasure, and the experience itself are transcended. Once we can look at an experience from these different perspectives, we can learn to direct positive healing energy to areas of difficulty. We can transform what is harmful into what will be helpful.

As we practice visualization, we experience 'direct seeing'. When we are relaxed enough, we can discover this 'seeing' through our immediate experience. This is done by loosening the muscle tension around the eyes, and without blinking, letting the sight become soft, like gazing. After that, for just a quarter of a second— observe. There is 'seeing'.

In consciousness, the senses are continually interpreting objects; but when the senses become lighter and more keen, not conscious of any particular object, then this becomes awareness. As this awareness is developed, the quality of 'seeing' naturally appears. Consciousness is a kind of looking, whereas awareness is a kind of seeing. The more we develop awareness, the lighter and the more sensitive its quality becomes. The more we develop sense-consciousness, the darker, heavier, and more depressed our awareness becomes.

In our lives we often experience a great deal of tension, guilt, and pain—the world may seem terrible, our jobs may be dull or we may have family problems or economic pressures. But as we develop our ability to *see*, each situation becomes increasingly interesting and workable because we can view it from different perspectives. Experience becomes more flexible, and we can open up our thoughts and find many valuable qualities within them. Ordinarily our thoughts are so subtle and fast that we cannot catch them, but once we enter this new dimension, we become more sensitive to this new kind of reality—we do not have to formulate it conceptually, for we can *know* it directly. In the beginning, this is really a fantastic discovery—from just one moment of awareness we can reach another energy level . . . a different universe. We can discover that the human mind has great potential and enormous resources—that the mind is our best friend.

Once we experience this for ourselves, we may wonder how we could ever have been so unhappy and confused. But we may still look at certain situations or problems in fixed ways—so we need to work this out. We know there is another way to look, to experience, to be. So why continue to spoil our present experience?

Once we can see the contrast between our old way of experiencing and this new open way, we can see how we have been deluding and confusing ourselves. As we develop awareness, we learn to let go of our habitual ways of dealing with situations; we see the old patterns begin to develop, and immediately stop them. Every experience becomes new—even though on the physical level our situation may not have changed.

Student: Are awareness and seeing the same?
Rinpoche: Yes. Eventually, as our understanding develops, everything fits a perfect pattern. 'Looking' and 'seeing', however, are different; 'being aware' and 'being aware of something' are also different. 'Aware of' is watchful—of thoughts, or tangible objects. Complete awareness, however, has no content. It does not contact anything—it is just perfectly aware.

Student: Is visualization a part of memory?
Rinpoche: On the relative level, time exists. On a higher level, there is no time. Awareness is a whole, like a ball—inside and outside, past, present, and future are all the same. So visualizations are not memories, but we may sometimes recognize or interpret them as such.

Student: I am not sure I understand the difference between conjuring up an image, retrieving a memory, and just 'seeing'. It all feels the same to me.
Rinpoche: One kind of seeing is based on past experience—perceptions, images, and memories. Another kind of seeing has no specific form—but then, memory images may mingle in. Whenever we think *of* something, we immediately create an image of the thought. The

thought and the image exist simultaneously—like a mother carrying an unborn child. We are all bound up with our memories, so 'seeing' may include many specific images based on our past experience. Generally, images obscure direct experience, inhibit the spontaneous flow of thought, and take positive energy from meditative states. But we can also transmute images by heating them up, boiling away their energy, and melting down their shape so that the form is no longer there. The images become pure knowledge, pure seeing, pure awareness. However, we may also 'see' without any images, so that our sight is transformed into awareness. That is, we penetrate the nature of existence—we go beyond time, and realize that past, present, and future are one. Once we understand this, we can understand how the mind operates.

Student: When visualizing an image, I experienced a strong smell of apple blossoms from my childhood. I wonder if visualizations don't also include feeling, touch, taste, and smell?

Rinpoche: Yes, everything. Still, I think perhaps you were picking up just the surface aspects without clearly picking up the background. While the smell may remain, you can also see your surroundings—the garden and the trees, the contour of the landscape, how you walked, or what you did in the morning and evening—memories you thought you had forgotten can come up.

Student: I tried once to visualize a flower and I had trouble seeing it. Then I thought if I lit a match, perhaps I could see it.

Rinpoche: But the 'seeing' we are referring to is not necessarily physical sight. 'Seeing' is: when you take away the rational mind and remain loose and balanced, then the experience immediately comes to you. Something is unusual. And that is the way to begin to 'see.'

Student: Could this be an awareness of sounds or other things around us?

Rinpoche: Yes, but awareness does not necessarily involve perceptual objects. The difference is, when we are 'aware of' a sight or sound, we are still dependent on the object, because of our association with it. This conscious awareness has a subtle grasping energy which supports the object we are conscious of—and thus holds us in bondage to it. We constantly lose energy in this process. However, when we are not aware of some *thing*, when we are just completely aware, our energy and knowledge are free and integrated.

When the quality of the visualization becomes very relaxed, 'seeing' will occur, although we will not necessarily see images. The seeing is the experience, not an interpretation of it. Once 'seeing' is a part of our lives, we continue to see the world around us, but we no longer hold on to the forms or images we see. Although this may not seem very clear to you now, someday you will understand—experience will speak for itself.

Student: Sometimes awareness seems to stop and become very quiet. . . .

Rinpoche: Right. This is the experience quality. Also, you may sometimes feel this experience quality when you are very angry or anxious, for at these moments the mind is very alert and whatever you look at is especially brilliant. At the moments when your awareness is one-pointed, negative forces cannot pull you off center. Awareness has a quality of wholeness . . . no one can divide it. It has a brilliant and perfect quality, like a diamond.

One type of exercise for increasing and refining awareness energy and for strengthening your meditation is to arouse anger without being internally caught by it. Certain compassionate deities may manifest terrifying, wrathful forms, but their inner attitude is always peaceful. A feeling can be very intense but with no agony or discomfort, no pain or separateness, no destructiveness or involvement associated with it. This flexibility is important, but in doing this practice for long continuous periods of time it is difficult to maintain balance; so it may be best not to do this exercise too often or for too long.

Each moment during the day there is emotion you can work with, and each situation is always very useful for renewing or recharging your energy. It is not a case of *reminding* yourself to be aware—the awareness is already there. You do not have to tell yourself about it, for once you do, you lose it. It is very difficult to be mindful all the time, but even when you sometimes forget, you can always begin again the next moment. The moment itself is the awareness.

The important thing is to try to be aware and flexible within each situation of your daily life. You may feel you should go on a retreat and *then* practice, but the teachings are not reserved for certain times. You can practice all the time—every aspect of experience is useful. There is no time to feel that you can put it off for awhile. Life itself is living practice.

Student: When you say that each thought is precious, do you mean we should not differentiate between thoughts . . . good, bad, or indifferent?

Rinpoche: Right. All our experience is valuable. We are already born into our true nature. Every single thought carries on the message, the power, the knowledge. Therefore, every single aspect of our experience is precious; there is nothing to throw away.

The mind produces a kind of motion as thoughts and images constantly move through it—and this motion produces a certain energy. We can also say that mind actually operates itself; the flowing is self-perpetuating. Furthermore, mind is not solid. It is not just an accumulation of perceptions or self-identities, but is a developing process—nothing watches from the background sending the mind messages—the mind operates without any basis, ground, or substance. It is nothing real in itself . . . the human mind can seem almost magical in its workings.

Visualization functions in a similar fashion. An image appears and we feel there must be something causing it to appear, but there is nothing. This is the magical quality of mind. Once we have seen this mind-power and are familiar with it, we can then direct it and use it for higher purposes. For example, when we utilize the water in a river, it can be very valuable for producing electricity; but the water itself does not have much value until it is harnessed. When we do not properly utilize the mind, we let the energy slip away. But when we use it properly, the mind reveals far greater resources than we had ever imagined were possible. Great potential exists within the human mind, but because our minds are very undisciplined, we can ordinarily interact with only one idea or image at a time. Visualization can be very helpful in channeling the energy and power necessary to exercise, strengthen, and develop the mind.

The best visualizations develop naturally. Once the visualization process truly starts to work, it is possible for a variety of natural phenomena to occur. Certain practices can produce very powerful effects, and some of these, if forced, can be dangerous both physically and mentally if we do not understand what we are doing. When these energies are not used in constructive ways, they will either simply stagnate and be wasted—even worse, they may do harm. So it is important to work carefully with these energies and integrate them so that they can actually nurture us.

The mental energy channeled through visualization is very powerful, and it may sometimes be very frightening. Certain fierce forms may appear before us—but these forms are not meant to terrify us, but only to teach us that the states they manifest are part of the nature of our minds, and that these states, when used properly, can generate positive mind energy. Visualization teaches us to use the entire mind.

Once we know how to use visualization, the visualization itself teaches us how to proceed. Explanations on the conceptual level are no longer necessary because purpose, value, and meaning reveal themselves as in an automatic feedback system. Visualization works naturally without the input of new information. The mind does not have to be told how to meditate or visualize; it is already doing so perfectly.

Meditative Awareness

Once we have touched meditative
awareness, our questions dissolve,
for both the questions and the answers
to them are within the meditation.

editative awareness has three primary qualities.
The first is calmness, the second openness, and the third harmony. As we practice meditation we naturally become calm, relaxed, and comfortable, and we find that meditation is very soothing and enjoyable.

Once we establish this basic foundation of relaxation, a quality of openness and acceptance arises which is free from doubt, worry, or judgment. We are not that much concerned with the 'meditation' and 'meditator', or 'right' and 'wrong' procedure. In this natural state of meditation no questions remain.

As we loosen our attachments and graspings we experience a feeling of clarity, harmony, and whole-ness—an awakened sensation which is very beautiful. At that time we can see our thoughts and emotions very clearly, yet we are neither distracted nor bothered by them.

Once we experience these three qualities of medita-tion we see their influence on every thought, word, and action in our daily lives; we have an 'awakened' feeling of joy, clarity, and fulfillment in a kind of true seeing. As we experience meditation, awareness increases and actually becomes a part of us.

In pure awareness our meditation is like the open sky—like empty space. There is no subject and no object. When we concentrate on particular objects, we relate to space in a dualistic manner—we look at objects through the mental patterns we have evolved to judge and discriminate our version of reality. These mental patterns set up a variety of subject-object relationships. Craving, grasping, and anxiety then come into being and give birth to the ego.

Pure awareness exists in the very first moment before these initial patterns arise. For example, when we wake up in the morning our sight, hearing, and touch perceive our environment very freshly and keenly. But then we make up 'sense stories', like children's tales. Our awareness asks, "To whom do these senses belong?" and suddenly we think, "Who belongs to this 'I'? Who is seeing, hearing, and touching?" We do not recognize that this is all part of a natural, integrated process. Instead, we interfere and say, "I see; I taste; I feel," and subjective conceptualizing begins. For that 'belonging-one' always needs someone or something to hold on to.

This is the very beginning of the ego. It starts with the establishment of the 'I' or 'self', which is not aware of its original state of being free from self; so with the ego comes separateness and dependency. Theoretically, this is how the ego develops. Practically speaking, what is happening is that every past moment is constantly being reinforced in the present, so the ego develops very strong habit patterns. And it continues to divide and separate experience until it develops a particular view of the world. Our sense perceptions then conform to this view, so that when we look—we no longer truly 'see'. We have difficulty getting back to pure awareness because we are controlled by our ideas, and the ideas create separateness. In other words, "Who is doing?" The 'doer-one' is 'me', 'I', 'self'. That self actually is a part of awareness, because it is manifested from within awareness. But we can no longer see the connection, so our interpretations and concepts produce a tight, limited mind.

It is not so easy to go beyond conceptualization and actually experience the non-discursive state. Mind or consciousness, is always relating to 'me'—to a subjective point of view. When we are meditating consciously, we feel that the instruction is coming to 'me' because 'I' am the meditator, or that 'I' the subject am within the meditation. We have difficulty accepting the fact that the way to meditate is simply to 'let go' of all preconceptions and expectations and to 'just be'. Once we can do this, we will realize that meditation is simply living in the present and not being concerned with past memories or future expectations. But we also need to be careful not to grasp at the present; we need to let go of any position, even the present position.

Wherever we are going, or whatever we are doing, when we cease grasping at our experience, we can develop our awareness, and unlock a vast storehouse of knowledge that will guide us spontaneously from then on. When we stop grasping at experience, we can transcend the ego, and thus experience awareness. Meditative awareness has no position, no 'belonging to' anyone or anything—neither to mind nor to consciousness. Awareness has no concepts and no instructions. It does not focus on any particular object. Within awareness we become free from even the 'idea' of meditation.

In our meditation we like to feel that we are doing something substantial, tasting a specific experience such as beauty, joy, or calmness. This attachment to experience ties us to our ordinary consciousness. So we need to get rid of this grasping—this collecting of experiences and commenting on them. We need to cut these very subtle levels of attachment and go beyond whatever position we are taking—beyond the senses, beyond concepts, beyond meditation.

Until we develop non-attachment we will always have to struggle with our concepts, our doubts and emotions, with questions of whether we are meditating correctly, making progress, or attaining enlightenment. Yet enlightenment never comes because we are holding on to our desires and expectations so tightly that our awareness is not free.

So, first it is important to penetrate our concentration and, as much as we can, to let go of even our very subtle mental attachments. When we experience awareness and let the natural energies of mind and body expand, then thoughts may appear—but they are part of awareness, so if we do not grasp them, they sparkle as they pass. We lose balance and awareness only when we become fascinated by these thoughts and grasp at them. Each time we reach out to a thought, we move farther away from awareness. It is like going out on the limb of a tree to reach an apple—when we go out too far, we lose our balance and fall.

So whenever any thoughts or judgments occur, we can just let them go; we can let go of the meditator, the meditating, and any meditated 'thing'. As we allow the positive energy of this natural state of mind to flow freely, our body energies also begin to move freely. At this point it is easy to meditate because there is nothing to practice, nothing to do, nothing to accomplish . . . there is just the fullness of being. Our experience is thus our meditation and meditation is our experience.

𝕎ithin awareness we can experience another realm, another kind of world. This is the beginning of the development of our 'psychic' potentials which are a natural part of our being. When we reach a certain openness, we may have unusual experiences which can frighten us if we do not know how to deal with them or how to go beyond them. It is possible to develop the potential for these experiences very quickly,

particularly when we contact certain energies correctly. So it is important to act with great care and to stay aware and balanced. Otherwise, we can be trapped in an experience or develop in an unhealthy direction.

At such times especially, it is important to have a teacher or a trusted friend who has experienced these levels and who can familiarize us with the path. There are certain instructions within the traditional literature which may be helpful, but each individual will have different experiences, and therefore the instructions will differ for each person. So we must be careful; we can become confused by our fantasies. If we want to 'fly', a good teacher can show us the map so that we can land in the right place.

At times, even when our meditation is going well, we may begin to worry that because we are not having any of these 'mystic' or 'psychic' experiences, we are not making progress. But we need not worry about seeing colors or images, or whether we can fly astrally through the universe, for these experiences are not very important, and actually may bring us trouble.

Experiences which are beyond our usual comprehension and which are quite beautiful, may occur naturally to certain highly accomplished meditators, or even to us. But they do not necessarily indicate that we are 'advanced' or 'spiritually evolved'. These experiences depend solely upon the qualities of our consciousness. Even when they occur naturally, if we become attached to such experiences, they can be a hindrance to genuine progress. We may not be willing to go beyond them. We may not even know we can.

The real test of our power and progress is our ability to transform our obstacles and emotions into positive experiences. As our daily lives become more balanced and negative emotions lose their power to distress us, the benefits and direct results of meditation begin to operate on very subtle levels. If we can handle our problems more easily, can balance our emotions and transform whatever is negative into what is positive and joyful, then we are truly getting results from our meditation.

The basic idea is that our meditation is everywhere. We can discover a kind of beauty even in our negative emotions, obsessions, or concepts—an inner beauty smiles on us and radiates from us. And who is the 'us'? The awareness itself. Before, we did not see or did not notice, but now we discover that awareness is already here. Every moment it is present, and our practice, our lives and work in the world become easier and partake of that quality of openness. We no longer perceive problems in our lives or meditations as insurmountable obstacles, and we may wish that we had known before that we did not have to struggle so much.

Once we have touched meditative awareness, our questions dissolve, for both the questions and the answers to them are within the meditation. For example, when we have never been to a particular place, we have many questions about it, but once we have been there our experience becomes the answer to our questions.

Even though from time to time we are unable to contact meditative awareness, we will never lose it, for we can always reawaken our awareness by letting go of 'subject' and 'object' and by going into our inner silence. There the deeper level of awareness develops naturally. When we experience these teachings so that we understand them within ourselves, and when we practice seriously and devotedly, then awareness is always available to us.

The more we develop this awareness, the more illuminating and alive it becomes for us. Thoughts no longer distract us; we can remain open, clear, and balanced. This penetrative, open quality is like the sunlight that shines forth in all directions. When we do not take positions, the door to enlightenment is completely open, and we understand quite naturally what is called 'universal' mind, infinity, or genuine understanding.

So once you understand even a little, keep going on, and you will find that your burdens become lighter and easier, and you will become more confident and open. Then you, yourself, become the teachings, for the whole universe is the awareness of your own mind.

Developing Balance

When we have meditative awareness
we know how to touch each experience,
and consequently we do not get
pulled in and trapped by expectations,
disappointments, or disillusionments.

From an ultimate perspective, there is only pure awareness. Awareness itself does not have any obscuration, so it accepts all patterns, all experience. As soon as 'experiences' filter through the senses, and perceptual patterns begin to accumulate, then all the images, memories, and reflections form what we call 'consciousness'. This is not to say that a substantial, original, or specific consciousness comes into being. We *think* there is a consciousness, but it is merely a collection of patterns which have accumulated like dust: this accumulation is what we call the 'self'. If we could sweep away all these patterns, so that the room of the mind were empty, we would not be able to find any consciousness at all. At the 'end' of consciousness, consciousness itself no longer functions. It is transcended. Only awareness remains —present awareness, which is always available within our bodies, within our energy.

Student: How do I know that I am aware? Will my feelings tell me?

Rinpoche: No. Feelings are within consciousness. There is awareness *within* consciousness—awareness of some *thing*—and there is awareness *beyond* consciousness. As long as we are aware *of* something, it is within consciousness—we are consciously aware of the existence of trees and mountains, and so forth. We organize our experience abstractly into certain patterns through words and concepts, images, and ideas, but the mystical or higher meditative state of awareness does not exist within consciousness. It goes beyond sense-understanding, beyond symbols, concepts, ideas. Without this deeper awareness we are still within the hold of our habitual actions, even though we may be experiencing very light, positive feelings within our meditations.

Student: I am rather puzzled, then, about the meditation that is focused *on* something, like a visualization, or directions from a teacher to meditate in a certain way.

Rinpoche: Visualization is one way to meditate, and very useful in the beginning. However, advanced meditators realize that no one is doing anything. This is what the directions are pointing out, and when we realize it, there is no need for directions, because we are already 'there'.

Student: What is the connection between 'concentration', 'consciouness', and 'awareness'?

Rinpoche: When we are concentrating we may be conscious but we are not aware. Consciousness without awareness is like milk with no cream, or like an orange with no juice.

Student: Can you have awareness without concentration?
Rinpoche: Yes. That is what we are trying to develop. First we concentrate; second, we are consciously aware; and third, our meditative awareness increases and develops until, finally, awareness is unlimited. It is very important to break down our conceptual building blocks, for, in a way, concentration builds a shell around meditation . . . something tangible or substantial with which we can associate. Direct awareness tries to penetrate the shell.

Student: How do we give up consciousness and still have awareness?
Rinpoche: We need to let go of any idea, any position, any concentrative quality that we are holding on to. We limit awareness by hiding in our thoughts. The danger is that all the images and spontaneous thoughts in meditation become so fascinating that we do not want to give them up; so we just stay within them, and we think that we are very powerful and have everything under control—*our* mind, *our* thoughts, *our* meditation. Certain visualizations and mantras help to build a bridge between consciousness and awareness, and thus help us to give up this kind of conscious meditation. Also, we can purify our body, speech, and heart by doing positive actions.

Student: Can concentration be a way of building our awareness?
Rinpoche: Gradually, yes, but it takes a very long time to build concentration solidly, and developing strong concentration does not necessarily mean we are also developing awareness.

Student: How will we know when we are meditating properly?

Rinpoche: The lower level of meditation is always involved with duality, with an 'I' who is aware of some 'thing', while the higher level of meditation is beyond consciousness. The distinction is between being aware of an object—categorical perception—and just being aware —intrinsic awareness. Consciousness collects mental impressions, while awareness does not. When we are still aware of thoughts, images, and objects within the meditation, we are still clinging to the sensory, categorical perceptions of consciousness. And as long as we are within consciousness, we experience various physical sensations, emotions, and interpretations: up, down; happy, unhappy; balanced, unbalanced.

Often, when we meditate, we may feel that we have fewer emotional upheavals or fewer disturbances and distractions. But this does not mean we are transcending the ordinary level, for past negative patterns still remain. Watching our thoughts, examining our feelings, and concentrating on refining our perceptions are temporary tools which can make us happy and joyful. But if we want to develop meditative awareness, we must transcend the sensory or intellectual awareness which focuses on objects. In other words, we must go beyond consciousness.

Student: How do you go beyond consciousness?

Rinpoche: Direct awareness! However, it seems that in meditating we always want to be doing something—to contact something substantial. We always want results . . . otherwise we feel our experience is not worthwhile. We may meditate for four or five years and find nothing tangible, and our meditation may seem dark, dull, and boring. We may become disappointed and stop medi-

tating. So this is a difficult situation—what we are looking for is what we are giving up!

Student: Do you mean that what we learn from meditation might cause us to give up our practice?
Rinpoche: What we give up is expectations. This can
upset us, as we usually feel that if we cannot possess
something, then it has nothing to do with *me*.

Student: Then what are the benefits of meditation if it has
nothing to do with *me*?
Rinpoche: The benefits are not tangible. They are found in
not taking positions, and in transcending the ego as much
as we can. Awareness is not some tangible 'thing', and
this special 'no-thing' cannot be held or pointed to. Even
nothing does not mean anything. Awareness has no
hands. If we speak about it, it is just noise. As we realize
this more deeply, we may suddenly think, "What am I
doing? There is no apparent value to being here." But
this attitude is unwholesome.

Student: Do *you* feel that way?
Rinpoche: I mention this because often people ask, "Have
you had any experiences?" We believe that having an
'experience' is very important, so we continually judge
our meditations, and nag ourselves about having an
'experience'. It can become a passion. We want to feel
pleasant, quiet, calm, and balanced. Some people feel it is
important to see visions, go to other realms, or communicate with invisible spirits.

Student: It's much nicer, say, than being depressed.
Rinpoche: Right. But when we go more deeply *into* the
meditation, these feelings are no longer present. The

more we experience the higher levels, the more we *become* awareness—the experience does not distract us. We do not pull it toward us, and we do not push it away.

Student: It's as though you are saying that if a person were to become enlightened, he would be disappointed.
Rinpoche: Exactly. I think so. We are disappointed because our expectations are not fulfilled. We have created and build up incredible fantasies—everything we could possibly imagine or hope for—but the more we develop higher awareness, the more we realize that these assumptions, dreams, and fantasies do not exist.

Isn't it dangerous to throw away our most cherished delusions? We may have been meditating one or two hours every day for six or seven years, and thinking that we were gaining something, but now we realize there is nothing to gain.

You might ask, "Why should I bother meditating? If meditation is not of benefit to my feelings, my perceptions, my bodily or mental condition, then what good is it?"

Student: Isn't it good for something?
Rinpoche: It can help us be joyful and relaxed. It can help us balance our bodies and minds. But, as we experience more deeply, we see that this higher kind of meditation simply *is*; it has no purpose in itself.

Student: So, why do you teach meditation?
Rinpoche: The purpose of teaching is to give people disappointment. People need disappointment! There is always disappointment if we expect something.

Student: I *expect* disappointment—I don't need that!
Rinpoche: That is the only way you can wake up. As soon as more disappointment comes, you can wake up.

Student: I should be very awake.

Student: It seems like a life full of love affairs would be easier than meditation.

Student: Life provides us with a great deal of disappointment.

Rinpoche: Right. A really good meditator is always learning, always working with disappointment. He knows how to deal with the world and with whatever experiences he encounters in his daily life—that is the *real* learning process. Really looking at our lives is the intelligent way to meditate, otherwise we just live our lives without benefiting from our spiritual understanding.

So, I am saying that meditation brings us back to life. We may have to struggle, but if we are determined to go through the obstacles rather than trying to escape or avoid them, we can experience everything—seeing, hearing, tasting, smelling, touching, and being aware —and dance with each situation rather than having to hide or protect ourselves from it. When we have meditative awareness we know how to touch each experience directly, and consequently we do not get pulled in and trapped by expectations, disappointments, or disillusionments. When we live this way we can find life very meaningful and valuable.

Yet ordinarily, we feel that dullness and restlessness are negative, while happiness and cheerfulness are positive. We are always taking positions. However, awareness is neither happy nor sad, neither positive nor negative. Awareness takes no position other than balance. For example, we can learn to shift very quickly between emotional states. For two minutes we can be angry, and for two minutes we can be peaceful. For two minutes, depressed, and for two minutes joyful, shifting back and forth many times from negative to positive,

positive to negative. Gradually we can develop such flexibity that we can be in either position easily. We are not fixed. Before we had no choice of how to be. Now we have a choice.

Student: Who has a choice?
Ripoche: Mind has a choice. If we are angry, depressed, or in some other emotional state, and can immediately change it, suddenly we are developing flexibility and balance. Usually, we just express the emotions, and become locked into a specific emotion, drama, or relationship. Then it takes a long time for us to calm down, analyze or digest the situation, and transform the experience into something more acceptable. But awareness is sharp. It is like an electric charge. We can instantly change any situation.

Student: Are you saying, then, that when a situation comes up, rather than just reacting to it, we should experiment with it? When somebody says something, we can get angry with it or be happy with it? We can experiment?
Rinpoche: Right. Experiment with your thoughts and reactions. You will find times when this makes you happy and times when it makes you upset. You may be hanging onto a certain self-image; or you may not want to honestly recognize a truth about yourself. You may find that you are not comfortable in quickly moving from one state into another. Perhaps it is difficult for you to become peaceful, and then when you become peaceful, you may find it very difficult to become angry, and very difficult again to become peaceful. So you sometimes need to be tough in penetrating your resistance. Carefully observe who it is that is holding back and what the

root of the blockage is. Practice shifting back and forth very quickly, exploring the opposite side.

Student: But what happens to the decision-making process? What shall I do with my life? What's the best action in a situation?

Rinpoche: Trust your awareness, and your body and mind will take care of themselves.

Student: You mean it doesn't matter what you do or what kind of work you are involved in?

Rinpoche: You cannot go wrong or be harmed, because awareness is like the sun, which always gives light . . . never darkness. Why is it so important to emphasize awareness? Because it does not collect emotions or obscurations, does not accumulate habit patterns, does not create suffering. Awareness is like the lotus—it has its roots in the mud, but the flower itself is always pure. So, as much as you can, increase awareness every day.

To develop awareness, first we have to know how to meditate properly. Second, we have to know how to go beyond meditation. And third—in more advanced teachings—how to give it up! When I say, "Give up meditation," I mean that you may have a conceptual *idea* of meditation. *That* is what you need to give up. I am not saying that you are not to meditate. You need to give up the conceptual idea of meditation, but continue being in awareness. Previously you may have meditated thirty minutes or an hour—morning and night—but now you need to meditate *all the time.*

Student: Are you saying that we should possibly give up other meditation practice?

Rinpoche: Yes, any time you identify with 'your' meditation. When you have feelings, notions, ideas, or concepts about meditation, you should give them up. Meditation has no structure—it is not 'yours'. In other words, when you develop awareness there is no longer any 'you'. Do you understand? Your awareness is disconnecting your ego.

This is the challenge. You do not need to make any extra effort. Just remain completely balanced in mind and body, and at the same time keep your awareness open. Meditation does not belong to your head—meditation is not an idea. Heads only create ideas, nothing more. On this awareness level, self-perpetuating ideas have no value, for you are within the thought—you become awareness. You continue to be entirely aware, but you are not necessarily even aware of that. Therefore, sit and meditate—that is fine—but you have to give up the concept or notion of your meditation. After you give this up, expand whatever is left, without holding it. This is awareness. Keep it alive by practicing carefully and skillfully every day. As awareness increases, nothing can limit you, not even meditation. In this way you can become completely open and balanced.

Part Five

TRANSMISSION

The Teacher-Student
Relationship

It is difficult to find a qualified teacher, and equally
difficult to accept the responsibilities of being a good student.
These do not mean simply to work hard, but also to
be receptive, open, and devoted to the teacher.

In the West there is great desire and esteem for knowledge; but what is meant by knowledge is usually merely scholarship—an accumulation of information which essentially ignores the understanding that comes from direct experience. The importance of the transmission of knowledge, linking teacher and student in a dynamic process, has essentially been overlooked. The attitude towards learning sometimes seems very mechanical—we pay a certain fee and expect to receive a clever perspective or two, or some useful 'techniques'.

The traditional teacher-student relationship, based on learning and sharing, sincere devotion and gratitude, has few proponents here. Students gather information from teachers who have themselves successfully gone through the same gathering process, and the only responsibility on either side entails an exchange of information. There is seldom any personal involvement on either side, and often both the students and the teachers forget about each other as soon as a course is over.

The tradition of passing experiential understanding from teacher to student has been all but forgotten here in the West, although this relationship did exist in some European esoteric traditions until a few hundred years ago. But once the link from teacher to student is broken it is difficult to mend, and experiential understanding is then hard to obtain. For although it is the natural state of mind, and there are thus rare occasions of contacting this awareness spontaneously, without a proper guide it is difficult to develop the foundation necessary to sustain, direct, and integrate such an experience into our daily lives.

Over the last few years, quite a number of teachers from various traditions have come to this country—and certain teachings seem to have taken root. In some ways the 'revolutionary' spirit which still is alive in this country has helped—there is an openness, an acceptance of different peoples and ways of thought. But 'tradition' is often looked upon with distrust, so even though much of the knowledge brought here by teachers from the East holds a certain fascination, there is a tendency to try to by-pass the traditional ways—and to try to obtain this new knowledge by using Western systems instead of the traditional methods, which often are considered irrational or inefficient. Or we may be so used to our scholarly approach that, even though we do not particularly like it, we are even more uncomfortable when we come in contact with the warmth of the traditional teacher-student relationship, that calls for a close link of mutual trust and confidence.

In Tibet there is a certain kind of deer that yields a

musk which is very valuable for making perfumes and medicines. Hunters go to great lengths to obtain this substance, caring nothing for the life of the deer. Likewise, students sometimes seem to value the teacher only for what he can give them—they think they can buy his head. But this attitude upsets the learning process, as the development of a wholesome relationship of mutual respect and appreciation is essential for both the student and the teacher. It is especially important for the student, because there is no way to attain genuine understanding except through direct experience—and this learning process needs the guidance of a teacher.

Often we try to collect teachings as we would collect stamps; we feel that by collecting a little information from here and there—something from Hinduism, Sufism, Kagyu, Nyingma, Zen—we are gaining knowledge. But just picking up random assortments of definitions, concepts, and techniques can be more harmful than helpful; fragments taken out of context often lose their meaning and can give us a distorted view of the teachings involved.

Teachers have different styles and personalities; they may not even agree with one another on the ordinary level—but that is all right, it may be even valuable. If there were no need for this variety, there would have been only one teaching and only kind of practice. But the student should not become fascinated with these differences or habitually pick and choose among the various teachers available, or even among the seemingly conflicting actions of the teacher he chooses. The main concern for a student is to cultivate a positive relationship with a teacher and to preserve it until full understanding unfolds.

So it seems important first of all to think very care- fully about what makes up a good teacher, and then be sure that the teacher we choose is someone we can trust, someone we can follow even if the way becomes more difficult than we expected. Following a teacher's instructions does not mean blindly accepting whatever we are told . . . but after taking the necessary time to carefully choose a teacher who inspires our faith and trust, it is important to maintain an openness to his guid- ance. We should be careful not to be limited by our preconceptions of how a teacher should be. External images often mean so much to us—we want our senses stimulated, or we want 'good vibrations'. We also want the path to be very pleasant and easily traversed. But a teacher, like a president, should not be chosen for his looks.

A teacher who we can trust to guide us well should have experiential realization of the teachings, fused with compassion. It is also important that he understand his students and really want to teach them, and that he be free from emotional or selfish motivations—for these can distort the relationship. In other words, he must know what he is doing.

A teacher must be balanced himself, so that he can give balance to his students. But many traditions tend to emphasize one aspect of training more than others. Often a teacher may not offer a well-rounded system of teach- ings—meditation may be emphasized without the nec- essary philosophical training, or scholarship may not be combined with sufficient practical experience to create balance. So it is important to consider whether or not a teacher places equal emphasis on both study and practice.

I t is difficult to find a qualified teacher, and equally difficult to accept the responsibilities of being a good student. These do not mean simply to work hard, but also to be receptive, open, and devoted to the teacher. Such qualities are not particularly encouraged in our Western educational system, so they are thus sometimes hard to sustain.

Great enthusiasm often motivates us when we first begin to follow a spiritual path, but often we do not have the necessary stability or perseverance to persist once the initial fascination fades away. We are lured to the lamp of the teachings, but we dart off when the warmth becomes uncomfortable. The novelty of the relationship may hold us for awhile, but then our great expectations are not fulfilled, or the teacher asks us to do something we do not like, or requires disciplines which seem to restrict our freedom. So we may tell ourselves that we have received sufficient teachings and break away— often to look for a new and 'better' teacher.

But when we leave one teacher because of difficulties in our relationship with him, it seldom helps to go on to someone else, for the difficulty we cannot reconcile is often only a manifestation of an obstacle in ourselves. Once we have assumed a trusting and serious relationship with a teacher, breaking it can result in much disappointment for both the student and the teacher. We may even become very bitter, feeling that the time we spent with the teacher was wasted. And a precious opportunity for growth can thus turn into a very negative situation. So once we have a teacher, it is best to firmly commit ourselves to that relationship so that we can make genuine progress on our path. In some ways it does not matter even how the teacher *seems*, for it is the *rela-*

tionship that counts. This relationship is unique; it is not like an ordinary social friendship that seldom lasts for long—it lasts until we attain complete enlightenment. That is its goal, and if we are to attain it, we must work to protect it. Our 'path' appears when we make this contact, when we come to the juncture in the road where we meet a good traveling companion.

Even if the teacher is somehow not right for us and seems to be far from perfect, when we remember that these distinctions are not as important as they seem— that all that truly matters is the chance to grow and learn—then we can use this opportunity to diligently study ourselves and see where our own weaknesses lie. And we may finally discover that we are the ones with faults, and that the teacher has been only showing us to ourselves. When we accept this and learn to trust in the teacher's advice—even when it is in conflict with our own understanding or desires—then the fruit of the relation-ship begins to develop, and real progress begins to be made.

An accomplished teacher can see in more ways than one—seeing not only present actions, but also their consequences. So when we follow his advice, even when we do not understand it at the time, later we may find that it was helpful to us in ways we could not have conceived of previously. At that time it may be hard to imagine how we could have ignored the help that the teacher was giving us—the new dimensions he was opening for us.

The teacher-student relationship can be the most stimulating experience of our lives, catalyzing and enriching a growth process in more ways than we thought possible. It can also encourage an open attitude, making it possible for us to receive all that the teacher has

to offer. Difficult tasks may be asked of us, but sometimes destructive habit patterns can only be broken by
great perseverance on our part. The teacher is there to
show us our potential and capabilities. When we finally
connect the teacher's advice with our experience, and
come to realize the value of his teachings, we will be able
to see ourselves more clearly and thus be able to work
with our problems more effectively. In looking in retro-
spect at our changes, we will be able to perceive the
teacher's ability to transform negative factors into what is
wholesome and valuable. So we should remain confident
in the teacher, and filled with trust; then real learning
—which often occurs in unexpected or disappointing
ways—can take place.

In the relationship between student and teacher,
there are external, internal, and secret teachings that can
be transmitted—all sewn together by the thread of the
relationship. Without contacting this lineage of teachings

in an intimate, personal way, it is very difficult to experience what 'realization' means. But once we do, we understand the kindness of the teacher—and a very fine relationship develops that is based on honesty, caring, and confidence. At this time compassion flows forth from our openness, and we begin to understand the responsibility we have to ourselves and others.

The teacher, the teachings, and we ourselves—are the foundations necessary for spiritual development. These three must be intimately linked for genuine progress to take place, and if any one of the three is missing, our growth is hampered. Together they are like good friends who trust and rely on each other. In order for the teachings to be transmitted we must remain open and accepting—like a white robe which is dyed the color of the teachings. Or, like film within a camera, we become transformed into the image of the teacher when exposed to the light of the teaching.

When the transference from teacher to student is full and open, we actually experience the teacher, the teachings, and ourselves as one. When we have this realization, it is as if we previously lived in a tiny dark room, with only a lantern for light; then suddenly were introduced to a vast, unlimited sunlit space. The joy and clarity of this experience make all the hardships of the teacher-student relationship worthwhile. The importance of this relationship cannot be emphasized enough. Unless the links to experiential knowledge are transmitted and carried on in this generation vast stores of wisdom will be lost.

Trusting the Inner Teacher

Ultimately, our best teacher is ourselves.
When we are open, aware, and watchful,
then we can guide ourselves properly.

Student: How can we develop the openness we need to find what is right for us as individuals? What will provide the catalyst to speed the process?

Rinpoche: Usually, we need a teacher, but a teacher cannot know what is right for us in just one or two weeks—it is a long, sophisticated process. First we may be given different exercises, for the teacher must know our consciousness, how our senses react. After practicing these exercises for some time, we describe our experience to our teacher and receive private instructions. Then, again we practice, and again confer.

A qualified teacher is necessary for our intuitive inner growth, since some things are difficult to learn without the guidance of one who has attained certain understandings and realizations. However, some teachers can know a great deal and still not deeply understand the minds and experiences of everyone; they may know some things about a person and yet not perceive the more subtle distinctions between each individual consciousness. The most subtle differences can only be seen by someone who is fully realized.

There is a system of mental diagnosis which can be used by the teacher to determine the specific needs of each student. Following this system is the authentic way for a student and teacher to proceed; however, in recent years, this very accurate method has seldom been utilized. Now, classes are commonly one or two hundred students, but a teacher cannot readily know his students without closer contact and interrelation.

Student: Do you think that it is always necessary for someone on a spiritual path to have a personal teacher?
Rinpoche: It is very difficult to generalize. Some people need the guidance of a teacher, but others may not. When we no longer have any delusions and can manage for ourselves, then we may not need a teacher, but until such a time, we should at least have spiritual friends who will help us.

The spiritual path has many obstacles, such as our inner dialogues, our feelings, our worries, or even our friends or families. So, good influences are crucial. Once we are interested in the spiritual path, associating with those of a similar nature can help support and protect us, and can create less confusion for us. A beginner has many problems, so it is difficult to keep the path in focus without such help. If we can take care of ourselves, that's fine, but until we can do this it is important to choose a supportive and harmonious spiritual environment. This does not necessarily mean that we should avoid the world—only that we should protect ourselves to a certain degree. As we develop our inner strength we may be able to take care of others as well as ourselves. However, working with other people prematurely may cause us to lose the strength we have gained, and may even bring us harm.

Unless we learn to protect ourselves, we will easily be tempted to resort to our past patterns and forget what we have gained from practice. We need to encourage ourselves and be strong. Self-discipline means 'right action'—that is, to do the best we can for ourselves. When our minds are not balanced, our actions will not be balanced, and we will go to extremes and create more frustration for ourselves and others.

One of the best ways to discipline our egos is to make friends with ourselves. When we are joyful, then the ego becomes calm and does not stir up frustration and discontent. We have problems because we *think* we have them, and since we *believe* in them we get caught in frustrating situations. Conflict occurs when we do not obey our own inner voice.

Student: Is there a point where a student should leave his teacher and be on his own even before his practice is completely developed?
Rinpoche: I think it is necessary, first of all, that we be able to manage in the world and not be deluded. Then, perhaps, we can leave. Once we know the essentials and are stabilized and confident, we can gradually evolve, and we can learn to grow from whatever mistakes we make.

Student: What is the difference between devotion and dependency?
Rinpoche: From an intellectual point of view, devotion is not considered a very high virtue, since most people do not realize or understand its psychological benefits. Devotion creates a responsiveness, as well as a power or energy, which, even though emotional, can be used to develop and increase awareness. Spiritually, devotion is

valuable because it expresses the aspirations and ideals of our inner mind; it creates an openness which is self-perpetuating.

Student: Is emotion sometimes a motivating force? Say we have a flame—if we blow a little air, it burns better. Emotion in this sense seems to be constructive.

Rinpoche: Right. That is why, in religious systems, devotion is felt to be so important. Although devotion is sometimes considered to be based on blind faith, and indicative of a lack of intelligence, devotion and prayer are very effective and powerful tools for generating and contacting more subtle levels of awareness. Through devotion the inspiration and teachings of the lineage are inwardly made known to the meditator.

Student: I notice that I am bothered by the idea of a teacher. I have been looking for a teacher, and I think I am looking for someone I can worship or venerate, someone who will fulfill all my desires. Could you talk more about the function of a teacher?

Rinpoche: Several hundred years ago the world had great respect for religion and spirituality, but when people became more scientifically oriented, this attitude changed. Everything had to be proven intellectually and scientifically, and since knowledge or understanding gained through intuition or faith is not scientifically predictable, faith and devotion acquired the connotation of weakness. So, these days, even an attempt at devotion causes us many internal conflicts. Total trust in someone else jeopardizes the ego's independence, and when this happens, the relationship between a teacher and student can be uncomfortable. We see that the teacher is treated as if he were somehow superior to the student, and this violates our feelings of equality. We do not see the value in this. But if a person is really qualified to be a teacher, we can gain a great deal through faith and devotion to him, and our trust is not misplaced. A qualified teacher takes upon himself the responsibility of guiding and inspiring our inner growth and development.

The relationship between teacher and student depends on mutual commitment and mutual trust. The nature of this relationship depends very much on us. If, in following a teacher, we think we are being manipulated, or being made a fool of, or if we think the teacher is playing games with us, our devotion may not be very healthy, since our spiritual growth depends upon openness and honesty. We want guidance, but we do not want to be told what to do—for that threatens our egos. We do not like being in a situation where another person seems to know more than we do. We want to have the feeling that we are learning by ourselves, so certain information or advice the teacher gives us, especially when it contradicts our own desires, may cause resentment toward the teacher and we may even feel like breaking our relationship with him. But if, through some unwillingness to face ourselves honestly, we do break the relationship of trust and commitment, it may be very difficult to make genuine spiritual progress.

There are some students who have great respect for the teaching, but not so much respect for the teacher. But it is important to recognize the teacher and the teaching as one. A student might wish to *try* to follow a teacher, and even make a commitment to see if it will work, but this attitude is not a sufficient foundation for beginning a serious relationship. It can cause both the teacher and student to waste valuable time. So it is important to develop a sincere commitment to a teacher, based on mutual trust and respect.

On an external level, the teacher possesses the inspiration of an entire lineage of past teachers, and this understanding is transmitted directly to the student. This idea of 'transmission' is like a printing block—once we carve an impression on the block it will print the same each time. This transmission has the power to charge us with a kind of electricity so that we become like 'light', and through it we can discover that we ourselves *are* the lineage. As the teacher transmits the teaching to the student, the student grows into the image of the teacher, until he becomes a teacher himself.

On a more inward level, 'teacher' means 'inner awareness', our own intrinsic nature. Our knowledge, realization, and daily experience can also be called our teacher—but even this requires the protection and inspiration of the 'real' teacher. If our hearts become open, then our devotion and compassion develop into a deep serenity. At that time the teacher may simply be a symbol for the positive energy which is freed when obstacles disappear and a rich inner experience automatically unfolds.

Because of our sense of inner truth we may yearn for a teacher who will give us realization of ultimate truth, but someone who never makes mistakes may be hard to find or may not be available. We may end up greatly disappointed.

So first we have to let go of our expectations. Once we open ourselves, we can more readily recognize the positive qualities of the teacher; and these qualities unfold within that open space, within our consciousness. So whether the external instrument of transmission is broken or is imperfect does not really matter. We can still receive a meaningful experience through working with that instrument. Once we have developed awareness within ourselves, then everything in our relationship with the teacher will appear to be appropriate.

Perhaps a teacher is only a catalyst, someone to point the way, to guide and even to push us to realize our true natures. The relationship with the teacher then becomes the total situation through which we grow.

Essentially, a teacher is a good friend, someone who can guide us and help us get out of troubling situations. In that sense everyone and every situation can be our teacher, friend, and guide, even though we must sometimes go over very painful or unattractive ground.

There is another aspect that may be involved here. Just as the world is mostly water, a human being is mostly emotional, and that emotional quality feels a need to be fed with joy or love. There is so much yearning to contact or be attached to others. We need support, we need to be fulfilled, but often we cannot rely on friends or lovers, society, or even our own parents. There is no one close enough to us to really fulfill us. We may have our friends and relatives and be very successful in business, but still not be satisfied within ourselves—because we are lonely. We crave fulfillment of our desires, and that craving itself creates an emotional flavor which affects whatever we do. So frustration and bitterness build up. When we stop reaching outside ourselves for fulfillment, then very gradually our desires begin to subside and we are less aggravated by our cravings.

When we are very sensitive, then transient and selfish 'loves' fail to satisfy us; we need to find someone we can truly rely on, someone we can love without fear of rejection. Then we can be free to act through our own understanding, our open hearts, our awakened energies. In this sense the teacher is a mirror of our higher self. He activates our source of inner knowledge and our sense of complete fulfillment. When we have an open heart, then the 'awakened experience' arises within us—we will know it, unmistakably.

Student: As a teacher, how can you help us develop our meditation after we learn to meditate properly?

Rinpoche: First of all, a teacher points out certain steps in practice, and encourages the student to follow, so that the student may gradually come to have the same experience as the teacher. This is the traditional way. Because he knows the area well, the teacher can explain the map and direct the student. The student's responsibility is to follow the map exactly. When he does not, then the experience or realization will not come.

Some people can contact the meditative state directly. They are completely ready to accept the teacher's directions. But other people are not able to follow instructions, or perhaps their desire to contact this state is not strong enough, so even though they read books on meditation, and practice every day, they still cannot meditate. When we can follow the teacher's instructions, we can see them as a kind of transmission that has a certain magnetism which helps us to understand. We can see that all ideas and theories are merely vehicles or instruments to aid understanding. When that understanding itself becomes illuminated and silent, there is no further need to question or to answer.

There are certain times or certain days when we are just naturally in the meditative state, and then there are no problems—meditation simply comes. At that time we can meditate well, and meditation itself takes care of us and becomes our teacher. Ultimately, our best teacher is ourselves. When we are open, aware, and watchful, then we can guide ourselves properly.

Other Dharma Publishing Books

Openness Mind by Tarthang Tulku. A sequel to *Gesture of Balance,* presenting more advanced meditation techniques.

Kum Nye Relaxation, Parts 1 and 2 by Tarthang Tulku. Over 200 exercises for relieving stress, increasing concentration, and revitalizing the body, mind, and senses.

Skillful Means: Gentle Ways to Successful Work by Tarthang Tulku. How to reawaken the joy of working and use inner resources to create a successful, meaningful way of life.

Time, Space, and Knowledge: A New Vision of Reality by Tarthang Tulku. Thirty-five exercises and a rigorous philosophical text reveal ever more brilliant times and spaces, opening new potentials for knowledge and human freedom.

Hidden Mind of Freedom, by Tarthang Tulku. Short talks on meditation, showing ways to develop mind's healing potential.

Kindly Bent to Ease Us, a translation of Longchenpa's poetical introduction to the Dzogchen path to enlightenment.

Calm and Clear by Lama Mipham. Translations of two complementary guides to meditation by a brilliant 19th-century Tibetan lama show how to build a stable, rewarding practice.

Crystal Mirror Series edited by Tarthang Tulku. Informative introductions to the Buddha, Dharma, and Sangha present Buddhist concepts, texts, lineages, and 2,500 years of historical development. Seven volumes published.

If you order Dharma books directly from the publisher, it will help us to make more such books available. Write for a free catalogue and new book announcements.

Dharma Publishing, 2425 Hillside Avenue
Berkeley, California 94704 USA